HOW NOT TO RUN FOOTBALL

Also by Derek Dougan

ATTACK!
THE SASH HE NEVER WORE
THE FOOTBALLER
ON THE SPOT
'DOOG'

HOW NOT TO RUN FOOTBALL

DEREK DOUGAN

ALL SEASONS PUBLISHING LTD
WOLVERHAMPTON

First published in 1981 by
All Seasons Publishing Ltd
13 Lower Green,
Tettenhall,
Wolverhampton,
West Midlands WV6 9AH

ISBN 0-907043-01-1

PRINTED AND BOUND IN GREAT BRITAIN BY
BUTLER & TANNER LTD
FROME AND LONDON

To the players and spectators,
without whom the game could not exist.

If you think you are beaten you are.
If you think you dare not, you won't.
If you like to win, but you think you can't,
It's almost certain you won't.

If you think you'll lose, you're lost.
For out of this world we find
Success begins with a fellow's will
It's all in the state of mind.

If you think you are outclassed, you are.
You've got to think high to rise.
You've got to be sure of yourself before
You can ever win a prize.

Life's battles don't always go
To the stronger or faster man.
But soon or late the man who wins
Is the man who thinks he can.

Introduction

Where there is no vision the people perish –
Proverbs

The people I have in mind are those who play football for a living and those who watch them play; footballers and spectators, dependent on one another and yet ill-served by those with power over them. The game's administrators and legislators are endangering the national sport by their reluctance or refusal to change direction and equip it for the needs of a society they prefer to think has not changed in half a century. They are rooted in the past, men without vision presiding over a system which, if it remains unchanged, will bring about the collapse of professional football as we have known it in England before the end of this century, perhaps before the end of the 1980s. On 21 July 1969, an estimated 500 million people watched on television the world's greatest scientific achievement, man landing on the moon. The following year one billion people watched on television the World Cup final in Mexico between Brazil and Italy. Britain shared the enthusiasm. Football fever followed England's 1966 World Cup victory, but throughout the seventies interest declined as the game became more stereotyped and great individualists were overpowered by systems and formations, reflecting the administrative attitude controlling the game. I am writing this book not for myself, but for supporters (present and lapsed) who have no means of expressing their views than in bar-room talk and in letters to sports editors. I am also writing it for the players, who are effectively silenced by their clubs and the football authorities, risking heavy fines and disciplinary measures if they speak their minds to the Press without club permission. Fans and players deserve and demand to be heard. I like to think that in this book I am their spokesman.

The fate of English League football is in the hands of 92 men. Not the chairmen of the Football League clubs, but 92 bank managers. It is they who allow clubs to run up massive overdrafts, it is they who allow them to borrow the money for sky-rocketing transfer deals, it is their indulgence which enables clubs to totter on. If they called in the debts and foreclosed, hardly a League club would be able to survive for another season. It is only the escalating value of their grounds, as assets, that keeps clubs in existence. Banks, being public companies, should be represented and be more involved in the running of football clubs. After all, they are allocating shareholders' and customers' money.

League clubs play the financial power game by using players as pawns, moving them about the country in transfer deals that have made footballers hyper-inflationary figures. Nothing else has increased in value so much as the footballer. Over the past 15 years, transfer fees have increased, soared well above the rate of inflation. But instead of financing clubs and giving them more security, the transfer system has had the opposite effect: it has brought many to their knees, begging bank managers to increase their overdrafts as they lurch from one crisis to a greater one, pleading poverty. Some bank managers are intimidated by club chairmen. I know of one First Division chairman who threatened to withdraw the accounts of fifteen companies, over which he presided, if the bank refused to grant a larger overdraft. The bank manager capitulated.

If the entire system is not overhauled and grounds turned into multi-sports centres with football as the nucleus, serving the whole community and not just a small section of diminishing enthusiasts, the game will finish itself off as a professional sport. Having been with seven clubs and the longest serving chairman of the Professional Footballers' Association in the post-war years, I am compelled to condemn a system which ignores the practical advice of numerous official reports into the state of the game. In this book I want to show how and why our football clubs have gone wrong and what they should do, not just for themselves but for the communities in which they exist but all too often disregard. I may be accused by the administrators and legislators of arrogance, but I am not writing for them. They never pay any attention anyway. If they did, football would have been changed long ago, in the wake of the Chester Report. They hear no wisdom, speak no wisdom and see no wisdom, even when they have commissioned it. They must be forced to change their ways, or we shall see clubs forced into liquidation, as supporters continue to desert them in the pursuit of other sports and recreation.

If at times in this book I am repetitive about certain issues it is because I want to emphasise the importance of changing the structure of football administration. I intend to keep on hammering points in the hope of driving them home, because if administrators and legislators are not goaded into action football will suffocate under their dead hands.

Football is not my religion, because religion demands an act of blind faith. I am, however, as devoted to it, with as much pride and passion as anyone can be to a religious cause. My mission in this book is to spread the gospel of football and to preach to those who have not yet been converted to the truth about the game, which has lost thousands of previously ardent followers. Why have they forsaken the game they used to love? Why do the game's legislators and administrators cling to Old Testament values when they should be expounding football's New Testament? The answers will be found in this book, which brings into focus my thoughts, feelings, judgments and visions of football accumulating over 30 years' experience of the game, at various levels, local and international. I do not claim to be football's Messiah, with all the answers for its deliverance. But I am convinced that proposals and recommendations outlined in this book could prove to be its salvation at a time when its death throes are beginning to be heard, even louder.

One

What is a football club? This is not a riddle, but it *is* a trick question. The trick is played on hundreds of thousands of football supporters, throughout the United Kingdom. They are tricked into believing that the clubs they support are run for them, that to all intents and purposes they are public football clubs, administered for their benefit by boards of directors. In fact, they are all private clubs, controlled by a handful of men, whose autocracy has become a stranglehold on the game and whose power is out of proportion to their knowledge of the game. They occupy positions for which they are not qualified. Most of them are more concerned with boardroom socialising and in promoting themselves than in looking after the interests of the fans on the terraces and in the stands.

Their motivation, for becoming directors of football clubs, has less to do with a passionate interest in the game and the welfare of those who play it, let alone the interests of those who watch it, than with social prestige. Of course, they are concerned about success, because success on the pitch enhances their social prestige. There are exceptions. I know some chairmen and directors – not many – whose devotion extends beyond personal grandeur. In my experience, they can be counted on one hand.

Boards of directors, who control the 92 league clubs – Nottingham Forest's committee is being reconstituted at the time of writing – have inherited a system they do not wish to change. And yet it *must* be changed. The entire system confronting professional football today is ruinous. Season after season the financial situation worsens and even the top clubs, Liverpool, Manchester United and Arsenal, are not only feeling the pinch; they are in serious financial difficulties. Many clubs throughout four divisions are on the edge of bankruptcy. Most are kept in existence through the indulgence of bank managers or by virtue of their grounds remaining valuable assets. Clubs are talking about having to disband fourth, third, or even reserve teams to economise. There is talk of clubs facing liquidation, and even the possibility of some clubs in the top and bottom flights of football, merging.

In this atmosphere of impending doom, woe and anxiety, club chairmen towards the half-way stage of the 1980–81 season held a seminar at Solihull in the West Midlands to discuss ways the game could be improved. All they came up with after their deliberations were recommendations to give clubs the freedom to play games between Friday evening and Sunday and a minor change in the points system. They denied they had met to discuss the 'crisis' affecting the game.

Reading reports of the seminar no one would have come to the conclusion that any of the League clubs were in trouble, at least no more trouble than could be put right by the Sunday fixtures.

The chairmen had an opportunity to examine the roots of the crisis threatening the foundations of professional football in this country and they turned a blind eye. They busied themselves with academic and irrelevant issues while they complacently ignored the underlying causes of the decline. Directors talk of the problems of hooliganism, the behaviour of players on the pitch, falling attendances and the media takes up the refrain. They do not talk about the most pernicious cause of the game's problems, 'the private club' mentality which puts an unbridgeable gap between club and supporters.

How often do directors mingle with the fans, to get to know their feelings and views? They sit stony-faced in their boxes when fans in the stands and on the terraces are shouting at them, trying to relieve their frustrations in angry chants and abuse. Then they, the directors and their mates go below to their well furnished boardrooms for drinks, sandwiches, cakes and all the other refinements supporters are denied, as they queue at overcrowded counters for extortionately priced cups of weak Bovril and over-sweetened tea and coffee in plastic containers.

Close to the halfway line of the 1980–81 season, John Parsons in the Daily Mail began a report headed 'Soccer's £8 m Drain' with the words, 'The fight for survival is on in earnest, especially among the smaller clubs, as Football League gates head for a catastrophic 4 million drop this season. In cash terms, that means a loss of up to £8 million.'

On the same day Manchester United, traditionally the best supported club in Britain, was said to be losing money after spending almost £4 million on players in the past three years. Mr Martin Edwards, chairman, said: 'Money is a big problem in the game today.'

The tragic irony is that he is both right and wrong. He is right because money is not coming into the game at a sufficient rate to stabilise the 92 League clubs. He is wrong because the problem is not the inevitable shortage of money, caused by falling attendances; the problem is the system which works against itself and prevents more money coming into the game.

The Peanuts cartoon below the Daily Mail article provided a perfect postscript. It showed Snoopy pretending to be a rattlesnake, saying to himself 'His victim will be petrified with fear' and adding, 'He'll be petrified because he knows there is no defence against a rattlesnake except for stuffing a blanket in his mouth.'

Football clubs are reacting to their financial troubles as if bitten by a rattlesnake they did not see coming. And while they are gnashing their teeth, the game's administrators and legislators do nothing to stop the poison from spreading. They have stuffed wet blankets into the mouths of those who, in official reports, have explained and described, in precise and clear recommendations, how the Football League clubs could get out of the present financial morass and prosper.

If the directors were forced to sit or stand with the fans on Saturday afternoons, they might be persuaded to pay more attention to the factors that have driven supporters away in their thousands and try to win them back. People do not stop going to football matches because they have lost interest in the game, though an emphasis by trainers and coaches on negative defensive tactics and unadventurous systems has undoubtedly driven away some of the old timers, with their memories of Finney, Mannion, Matthews, Lawton, Law, Best, and Greaves. They stop going because they feel the clubs are treating them with indifference or contempt. They are being asked (not asked, *made*) to pay more and more at the turnstiles for less in amenities and comfort. They are shuffled in and out, with little or no concern for their interests. 'Pay up, watch and get out,' could be the slogan of any club in the Football League.

While the present system remains and perpetuates itself, the game will continue to decline, as supporters drift away to find other diversions. The local football club, usually built in the backstreets, shared with the music-hall a community's social focal point. Football was an 'artisan' sport, working-class to the core. Footballers and supporters were on equal terms. Quite often they met at the same bars. There is a theory, advanced by one or two 'enlightened' managers, that the ending of the maximum wage in the 1960s ended this relationship, by enabling the players to desert the pubs in favour of trendy nightclubs. But who do we see in these nightspots? Not just footballers; they are full of young people, earning good wages, who can afford the price of a season ticket or a seat in the stands. And if we pause to ask them: 'Do you support your local football club – and if not, why not?' they would probably say: 'That draughty old place? Go through the turnstiles like cattle and what do you get out of it?'

What does the fan get out of football today? Very little. The die-hards will always be there, but they are a diminishing breed. The 'floating' fan is hard to condition into the football habit. He may go occasionally, for a big match; otherwise, he will decide that going to a ground, Saturday after Saturday, smacks too much of the old working class and has failed to move with the times.

Supporters want to belong to modern times, not to be thrust back to a Victorian-Edwardian twilight world of artisan pleasures and backstreet folk customs. They look on football club directors as remote figures in suede shoes, fur-lined overcoats and forever puffing on fat cigars. A caricature, perhaps, but embedded in the minds of people whose own involvement with a football club can never, under the present system, extend beyond the stands and terraces for 90 minutes on Saturday afternoons.

Football has failed to keep pace with social change. It has an antiquated image and an idea of itself which no longer attracts mass public support. Boardrooms remain the bastions of privilege, reflecting the self-interest of a few at the expense of the many.

If football is to survive and progress, radical changes must take place. For a start, I would make it a condition of appointment for a director in the First Division to contribute the sum of £50,000 interest-free as evidence of good intent and seriousness. I would set the capital contribution for a Second Division director at £30,000; the Third Division at £20,000 and the Fourth Division at £10,000. By this means directors would be sobered up to the financial realities of running football clubs. Having put in their own money they would have to take a much closer interest in their clubs' financial affairs. There would be no reduction should a club be relegated. If a club won promotion I would expect directors to increase their contributions accordingly, because the emphasis for any ambitious club must be on promotion, not relegation.

I believe this condition of becoming a director would sort out the genuine directors from the dilettantes. There are too many football directors whose only interest is the social prestige which comes from sitting on the board and being seen in the directors' box.

The sums to be invested would balance with the value of all the perks and privileges that go with directorships. I know of directors whose shareholdings are no more than £60 and £70, but they enjoy perks worth thousands of pounds a year, I also know of a couple of directors who would resign if they had to put up £5,000. Directors can get in free at any of the 92 League clubs, where they are entertained in the boardrooms. They enjoy free travel with their clubs, often to distant parts of the world, and on top of this they can claim daily allowances while on tour. In the First Division I would assess the perks are around £20,000 a year, on average, not bad for an 'investment' of less than £100. Directors should put their money where their mouths are, but I'm afraid that because of the vested interests in the status quo, change will have to be forced on them. They will no more change the system of their own accord than cut their own throats. Ironically, they are cutting their throats in a sense, by squandering resources and lamenting falls in attendances instead of re-developing their grounds to meet popular needs and bring in more money.

Extravagance and a dogged refusal to help themselves, as they cling to outmoded conventions reminiscent of Victorian and Edwardian attitudes, have brought League clubs to the edge of disaster. For all the good they are doing in these desperate circumstances, boards of directors might as well be replaced by hordes of lemmings. There are times when I really think they have! It would be unfair to say that clubs and their boards have a suicidal urge or a death-wish, but they give an impression of floundering helplessly against prevailing currents and the winds of ill-fortune when, with more imagination and effort, they could be building new grounds improving facilities and planning for the future without getting hopelessly into debt. I recall one bank manager telling me that he had seen stable, business-minded company directors become irrational, over-emotional and unstable when serving as directors of football clubs. I had to admit this was my impression too!

Isolated from the running of his football club, the average supporter is left in the cold and many are reacting by staying away.

In the 1948–49 League season, matches were attended by 41,271,414 spectators; that is, those who paid at the turnstiles or had season tickets. Since then, attendances have not so much declined as slumped by some sixteen million. Five million have gone in the past ten years, including well over two million from the First Division. As I write this, glancing at the attendance figures alongside the results – Stoke, 13,079; Coventry, 12,255; Wolves, 20,699. In the Second Division only three clubs, I notice, have produced attendances in five figures.

The 1980–81 season was scarcely in its stride when Ipswich chairman Patrick Cobbold was predicting a further decline of 20 per cent.

Nothing delights the media more than such chilling statistics, which enable them to interview the woe-begonners, the analysts and commentators, the pundits and prophets of doom, all with their own explanations for 'what has gone wrong'. One of the more specious arguments, advanced by Watford's articulate young manager, Graham Taylor, is that players and spectators who used to be 'at one' are now socially poles apart. He reasons that terrace crowds, in their cloth caps, used to identify themselves with the players, whose wages were much the same as their own. Socially, they were on the same level and met in clubs and the pubs. Then came 'the revolution', the ending of the maximum wage and before you could lift a pint of beer and say 'Cheers' the players were patronising the new lush night-clubs while the terrace supporters clung to their working-men's clubs and pubs. He believes the ending of the maximum wage should have been introduced more gradually, though how you end such a system 'gradually' he does not explain. You either end it or you don't and it had to end, if footballers were to be treated like ordinary men on the terraces and not as playthings to be set in motion on Saturday afternoons.

While it is true that a number of footballers today earn a lot of money, and a few stars of the game can double or treble their salaries by endorsements and various commercial contracts, it is not true that all footballers are doing very nicely and living off the fat of their clubs.

I doubt if more than a few players, at one or two of the most glamorous First Division clubs, enjoy luxurious life-styles. For every Trevor Francis, Peter Shilton and Kevin Keegan there are a hundred players worried about paying their mortgages and their fuel bills. The big-money boys get the headlines and a misleading impression is given that all, or most, footballers are getting inflated wages and this is a drain on the game's resources, which accounts for the parlous state of the game and so on and so forth, *ad infinitum*! It is always worth remembering that without the players there would be no game!

While this sort of simplistic explanation for the game's decline is put forward, and seriously discussed, it will continue to decline – because the real causes of the game's decline are being overlooked or ignored.

It is as if there were a conspiracy to discourage a proper examination of the ills that have befallen the world's greatest team game, as administered and played in Britain. What is worse, I detect a malignant, malodorous attitude by those who have the power and authority to put matters right but who remain silent or attribute the malaise to causes beyond their own jurisdiction. One day we are told that crowds are staying away because of hooliganism. But when we examine this argument we find that the much-publicised hooliganism is confined to a small number of clubs and that attendances have slumped even where no 'football hooliganism' has ever been reported.

Then we are told that players' behaviour on the pitch is

responsible for brawls and violence on the terraces, whereas most hooliganism takes place in the streets before and after matches. And how often are players seen squaring up to one another on the pitch? What is really meant by 'players' behaviour on the pitch'? Most bookings are for minor infringements and a majority of sendings-off are for being booked twice in a game, not for giving practical demonstrations to yobs on the terrace of how to biff-and-butt a rival. The game is cleaner today that at any time in its history. This statement will surprise a lot of people but it is manifestly true.

While we busy ourselves with dramatic but irrelevant arguments and mistake symptoms for causes, the game will hurtle along towards oblivion. It is in a bad way, from top to bottom, from the administrative heights to the depths of the Fourth Division.

Spectators complain that the game itself has lost its sense of adventure and has become too negative, obsessed with the numbers racket – four-four-two, four-three-three formations. One manager has said he is not concerned about entertainment value, only about winning. A former star player, Malcolm Macdonald, now manager of Fulham, says the most important people in the game are the players. A former star manager, Stan Cullis, replies that the most important people in the game are the spectators.

Both are right. The point is that players and spectators are inter-dependent. Players can perform without spectators, as the West Ham team had to do in its European Cup-Winners' Cup match early in the 1980–81 season, but there were plenty of spectators for the TV coverage and it is unthinkable to contemplate football without spectators as it would be to stage a play without an audience.

What does a spectator hope to get for his support at a football club? All he gets is the opportunity to endure antiquated conditions that are a total disgrace to the administration of the game. Britain is the only place in the world where you pay your money to be a season-ticket holder in an environment which fails to eliminate or adequately control hooliganism. A small band of people have absolute control and have so many vested interests that they will not change their attitudes towards running a football club on the lines of a community centre, developing facilities all the community can enjoy, within a multi-sports complex. The cardinal sin of the legislators is that they have not taken any notice of the reports published since the middle of the sixties, a terrible indictment.

If spectators turn away in ever increasing numbers, as they have been doing in recent years, the causes have to be identified and measures taken to lure them back. Where do they go instead on Saturday afternoons? Shopping with their wives? Do they stay at home to watch Grandstand and World of Sport? Or do they kick their heels, wishing they had not broken the football-going habit, but knowing that the game had lost its interest and they could no longer afford the £1.50 to stand or £4 or so for a seat?

Football clubs have only themselves to blame. They could have reversed the decline if they had taken stock of the game, at all levels, and agreed on measures to counteract the rot once it had set in during the early seventies. Complacently, they exploited the euphoria which followed England's 1966 World Cup win. In the reflected glory of the event, they enjoyed a renewal of crowd interest. Football was again exciting. People wanted to share the excitement of victory and did so in the only way they could, by going to football grounds. There were subtle and psychological reasons for this mass reaction to the winning of a cup.

Britain by the mid-sixties had lost, or surrendered, its Empire. The austerity of the war years had given way in the sixties to a feeling of buoyancy, hence the phrase 'the swinging sixties'. There was, however, a vague feeling that it was all illusory. The Macmillan years of 'never had it so good' produced, in the background, a sense that the country was deceiving itself. How could Britain, without an Empire, this continental off-shore island, remain a power in the world? We were, perhaps, just swinging along more in hope than in expectation. When Sir Alf Ramsey's re-modelled England side won the World Cup the ecstasy went beyond the mere winning of a football honour. It was felt in every home in the country, as a sign that Britain was, after all, still great and could match the best in the world. Not only match it, but beat it. We could beat the new emergent power, West Germany – the country financed and made secure for democracy by the powerful United States.

Unaware of their own failings and deficiencies, League clubs enjoyed a false boom. When the euphoria had declined – in the words of the old hymn, throbbing hearts soon sink to rest – the scene changed. Since those heady times the international side has faltered and undergone tensions and changes. Once the glow of winning the World Cup had faded, crowds began to desert the stands and terraces; not *en masse*, but gradually.

People get a strong stimulus from the success of the national team. When it is performing wonders they register their excitement by taking a closer, even a more passionate interest in their local League clubs. The glory rubs off, down the line in the League. But if it is not doing anything spectacular and promising more than it achieves, disenchantment brings with it fading interest in League football. A dramatic illustration of cause-and-effect came with England's performance in the Nations Cup in Italy in the summer of 1980. The sporting Press had given us the impression that all the England side needed to do was turn up and go through the motions. The Cup was as good as ours, the play only a formality. The build-up was overpowering and in the event, deceptive.

England's failure, coming after corresponding failures in the World Cup since 1966, had a depressing effect and I believe has been partly, or even largely, responsible for the slump in attendances at League grounds during the 1980–81 season.

The big question now is: can the decline be halted and reversed? If I did not think so, I would not be writing this book. The tandem question is: how should football be run to bring back the crowds and make it a mass attraction? The title I have chosen, How Not to Run Football, may seem negative, but it is important to show what has gone wrong with the game before showing how it could and must be put right. The cause of a disease has to be identified and the symptoms isolated before a cure can be found.

My track record in football management has been confined to two seasons as chief executive of a non-League club. Am I then presumptuous in writing this book and over-reaching myself? I have had more than 30 years' experience of football, from the grass roots (or more correctly, the scrub and wasteland of East Belfast) to the high realms, from youth club football to international competitions. As the longest serving chairman of the PFA since the Second World War, I had dealings (and some wheelings) with the game's leading administrators. For more than three years I was the PFA's main negotiator with the football authorities for freedom of contract for players. I was still chairman of the PFA and there were two years to go in the negotiations when I went to Kettering.

Although Kettering Town in the Alliance League is a small club, with part-time players, it is (or was in my time there) in some ways representative of the organisation of any League Club. What happened at Kettering on a small scale had its counterpart on a broader scale at a First or Second division club. Basically, the set-up was much the same and I gained astonishing insights, causing me to investigate further and wider the administration of the game.

I have since discussed with chairmen and directors how their clubs are run. Some have been defensive and non-committal, others forthright and honest. The overriding impression I have of the average board of directors is that they regard their clubs as private clubs, for their own social prestige and local prominence. Naturally, they would never admit this in public or even to their relatives and friends. They convince themselves that they only have the public interest of their clubs at heart, but how many are prepared to step down when their clubs are languishing and facing relegation? How many, on sacking their manager, sack themselves with the proper acknowledgment that they too are responsible, because they appointed the manager, so their judgment was at fault?

Sometimes they fight among themselves, in their inner sanctums. They blame one another, organise their own conspiracies and when it gets into the newspapers the phrase used is 'a power struggle'. 'The Battle of Villa Park,' with knives out in the boardroom, was a typical example.

Rarely, if ever, are supporters asked to deliver judgments, if only through supporters' clubs, which some clubs refuse to acknowledge, fearing that the very people on whom they rely at the turnstiles might become too influential for their (the directors') own good. I have heard many a director say: 'We don't want them interfering and trying to tell us what to do. Running a football club is not their business.' Whose business is it anyway?

In my view, professional football should involve the local community, representing the public interest. I would like to see League clubs run in conjunction with local councils, with grounds developed to serve the community at all times of the day, with the football club retaining overall control. A government White Paper suggested this in 1975. It might as well have been 1875 for all the consideration given to it by the game's legislators.

Football would then be a nucleus of a ground, converted into a multi-sports centre, with the emphasis on family recreation and participation. This is what I had in mind at Kettering, which could have been a prototype for other clubs to emulate. For various reasons, which I shall enlarge on later in the book, ambitious plans were stifled. The scheme never got off, or on, the ground and an opportunity was lost to set a lead for clubs throughout the country.

Perhaps not 'lost', only delayed. If football is to save itself, it will have to free itself of its Victorian image and the lethargy which has enfeebled its administration in the past, and equip itself to move towards the 21st century with stadiums designed to cater for shorter working weeks, far greater leisure and activities which at present only a few enlightened civic authorities provide.

Time is not on football's side. In the circumstances, with so many reports and statistical surveys underlining the gravity of the situation and pointing towards disintegration after a prolonged period of stagnation, one might reasonably expect 'all hands to the pumps'. Instead, we find administrators and legislators 'washing their hands' at the pumps, glibly talking about things coming right in the end and going back to their boardroom cigars, whiskies, and gin and tonics.

Ah, yes, all very well, say the sceptics and cynics. But these are difficult times and money is scarce. But is it? A short while ago I picked up a magazine and read an account of the life and lucrative times of a racehorse owner, Robert Sangster, who had switched £8 million investment in second-hand cars to thoroughbred yearlings. I am not concerned about his investments or his sporting interests. What interested me was the source of his income. At 44, he is a multi-millionaire, who prefers to live on the Isle of Man. His fortune had come from Vernons football pools. In five years he is reputed to have spent 20 million dollars in his quest for the perfect yearling. What he does with his fortune is his own business, but it indicates how much money is made by the pools firms. The pools firms make their fortunes out of football – and what does football get out of it? A minimal amount. The Moores family has diverse money-making interests stemming from the pools. Without football, they would have few or even none.

The government could easily direct a greater percentage of pools earnings to go into the game. Its grant to sport for the 1976–77 season was just over £10 million when the Arts Council grant was £30 million. For 1981–82 the Arts Council grant is £77.75 million. More than a quarter of the country's population engages in sport – about one per cent has a direct interest in the arts. Why should sport not get at least an equal share with the arts?

The Central Council for Physical Recreation not long ago estimated that sport needs another £25 million each year to provide adequate facilities. It should be remembered that without proper back-up in amateur sport and football in particular, there is no chance that we will compete effectively in international competitions on the professional level.

Football, as the national sport, continues to get a raw deal while the pools firms continue to heap one fortune on to another, season after season. They could afford to be far more generous towards the game which provides their fortunes. After all, they have a vested interest in the well-being and future progress of football. They should be anxious to invest adequately in a profession which is their be-all and end-all.

Is our Minister of Sport taking measures to provide a greater allocation for funds to football through the pools firms – or is he merely sitting back, like his predecessors, watching the way the wind blows, when the winds of ill-fortune are tearing away at the fabric of professional football in this country?

Two

Why do I harp on the reports commissioned to help football to survive? The Chester Report, shamefully and flagrantly pigeon-holed, was appointed under Norman Chester, Warden of Nuffield College, Oxford, in June 1966, to enquire into the state of Association Football at all levels, including the organisation, management, finance and administration and the means by which the game could be developed for the public good - and to make recommendations. *The Football League and the FA were concerned about the deteriorating financial position of the game and the need for money for its improvement and administration.* A levy board, on lines similar to the Horse Race Levy Board, was suggested as a means of raising money.

Though the Chester Committee was reporting to the Government, most of its recommendations were addressed to the various bodies responsible for the running of the game. The establishment of the enquiry was welcomed by these bodies and the committee had the fullest co-operation from them. '*The future of the game lies in their hands,*' declared the committee, in presenting its report.

The Chester Committee – whose report became my football Bible - recommended that a levy of one per cent should be made on the gross proceeds of all pools, after the deductions of the Pool Betting Tax levied by the Government. It would be levied on all football pools, not just those managed by the Pools Promoters Association. It would be easier and cheaper to levy than the racehorse levy, for the Customs and Excise Department already had all the necessary information in collecting the levy of 25 per cent made by the Government. In the year ending 31 March 1967, some £122 million was staked in football pools out of which tax of £30.5 million was paid. In that year, the new levy would have raised £915,000. The Board of Customs and Excise estimated a ten per cent increase for 1967–68, so that a one per cent levy should produce about £1 million. Today we could have argued strongly enough to get £20 million.

If the constructive proposals made by numerous committees had been implemented, football would have begun the 1980s without financial worries. The Football League would have been secure, down to the smallest lower division clubs and there would have been no desperate talk of one club trying to buy another, or a non-League side like Scarborough trying to buy and take the place of another, Halifax Town.

Football has missed a great opportunity by not implementing the recommendations made by official government enquiries, all of them now a waste of time and money. It amounts to a dereliction of their duty as administrators of the game not to act on recommendations made by impartial, unbiased committees in the interests of the game. Why didn't clubs activate these various reports over the last 15 years? It is simple. They would have had to change their whole conception and their whole attitude of running the game and they would have had to give up their stranglehold on the game. As I have often said it is easier to penetrate the Mafia than to penetrate or to get involved with the Football Association or the Football League, because they are the most watertight organisations and private clubs in the world.

Regardless of how much talent and ability, how much enthusiasm and how much energy anyone is prepared to contribute and regardless of how much experience and how much money a person has, you cannot get in unless a few select people agree that you are a fit member or you are capable of becoming involved in the running or day to day involvement of a football club. Football clubs have missed an unique opportunity to help the youth of Great Britain. They could encourage them to behave properly by instilling more discipline and giving them the opportunity to develop their aspirations, in sport. They have failed the footballing public while drawing on the goodwill of the footballing public. Is it to be wondered why there is now a lack of response from the public? I am continually asked by people, 'Why is it there is so much trouble at football grounds?' If parents knew that grounds were developed in such a way that there was total supervision and no risk of youngsters being involved in any sort of incident or fracas, and at the same time they could play a game of squash, a game of badminton, 5-a-side, enjoy proper training, or go on to watch the football team, I believe attendances would increase tremendously. Money would continually come into the game, to keep improving facilities and develop the stadiums to meet the aspirations of the entire community. The more you can occupy the minds of young people, the fewer will be the problems of boredom. They would think less of the seamier side of life, such as taking to drink, smoking, or taking to drugs. It has been conclusively proved that The Beatles and The Rolling Stones and other outstanding performers, pop or in sport, set standards and habits which youngsters emulate. This is one of the main causes of concern, as I speak to schools, referees' associations, Round Tables, Rotary clubs and other organisations. Questions come round to the behaviour, or the standards of behaviour, set by their idols. People in the public eye should set a better example for youngsters to aspire to. The behaviour of so many public people over the last three years has certainly left a lot to be desired, including politicians. The irony is that there is money available if only football clubs would grasp the opportunity and approach the Government in such a way that money would be made available for them to bring their antiquated grounds out of the 19th century and into the 20th century. If they do this, there is the possibility that they could bring their thinking into the 20th century as well. I am sad to read and to hear of the continual squabbles that television doesn't pay enough money, the Pools Organisation doesn't pay enough money, but if football clubs had recognised 20 or 30 years ago that they had the most marketable sporting product ever produced to make money and to continue to make money, we wouldn't be talking about such petty issues as too much football on television and the silly matter I had so much trouble about, putting the name of a sponsor on a shirt. So much money could be coming into the game that one should not need to resort to having a sponsor for such derisory sums. The Government could and should be chipping in at least £20 million per year. The government takes out of football in excess of £150 million a year in tax. What other industry in the United Kingdom, employing 2,500 workers, generates this sort of money for the Treasury?

The football industry has every right to ask for some of this money back. Of course if you gave the people running the game that sort of money what would they do with it? One of our fears at the PFA is that they would spend it on transfer fees for footballers, and not on their grounds and the community. A Labour Government's White Paper back in 1975 recommended that football clubs and local authorities should get together and develop grounds in the interest of spectators. Six years later, this hasn't happened, and it will never happen if the vested interests of directors of football clubs are not swept aside. Sport and recreation can play an important role in the lives of families. If football clubs were developed on these lines, I am now suggesting entire families could be members of a football club. The people who run our game are devoid of ideas and if they do have ideas they don't know how to implement them. I remember going to one ground where an official – and he is one of the bright ones – took delight in showing me around the ground and explaining how they had built the new boxes for a handful of people to enjoy luxurious facilities. They had also built a big new stand and developed their old stands. I said that if I had my way I would demolish the lot and start again. He was taken aback by my statement and said, 'What do you mean?'

I said, 'I mean, they only enjoy all this less than 25 times a year and only from 2.00 pm to 5.00 pm on Saturdays which if you work it out, is less than 80 hours a year, and if you work out how much you are paying in rates and everything else on the upkeep for those 80 hours it works out as very costly indeed. If I had my way I would demolish the whole lot and start again and implement facilities the entire community could enjoy.'

He left me aghast because he thought I was a raving lunatic to make such a suggestion, when they had spent so much time on the development of the ground. It is just a monument, a big empty place to which a few thousand people come every other Saturday, just to stand on the terraces or sit in the stand and a couple of hours later they go and are not seen again for another fortnight. Unless of course, they are trying to recruit agents and are making appeals for support to sell more tickets to raise more funds to be squandered and to implement facilities not intended for all the public. This is why I am against the system. A system that can be perpetuated like this is not in the interests of everyone, only in the interest of a handful of people. Anyone who makes such a categorical statement and castigates the system and those who administer it, is regarded as a trouble-maker, a radical or a non-conformist. The irony is that I am not rebellious and am only agreeing with the reports written and published over the last 15 years. It is all there for everyone to read and digest. This is why I have tried so far without success, to acquire my own football club and develop it in the interest of the entire community. A football club should be developed so that children, even in school holidays, have the opportunity of being involved, to have a sense of commitment and know that the football club cares for them and considers their interests. Instead of doing all they can to generate goodwill among families, local authorities and the community, the football authorities devote their time and attention to other concerns. They are 'sissies', by which I mean they are playing out the ancient myth of Sisyphus, a legendary king of Corinth, crafty and avaricious, whose task in the world was to roll a huge stone up a hill until it reached the top. As the stone constantly rolled back, his work was incessant, misguided and foredoomed. Football's legislators and administrators are engaged in the hopeless and meaningless task of pushing uphill the deadweight of a system which has for long outlived its usefulness. It keeps rolling back and sooner or later it will roll over them all, unless they use it as a marker, signifying the past and the way ahead.

Gone are the days, with the exceptions of Liverpool, Manchester United, Tottenham, Aston Villa and Arsenal, when you can expect crowds of well over 35,000. The leading bodies should have accepted the recommendations of the Chester Committee way back in 1968. If they had implemented all of their recommendations we would have had so much money coming in annually from the Government, a full-time supremo could be appointed with absolute control to scrutinise football clubs and advise them on developing their grounds, providing in most cases all-seating, and establishing other facilities, so that youngsters had the opportunity to support their club, meet their heroes and be involved with them, hopefully learning from the players and enjoying recreation in its full sense of the word. Football clubs are too remote from their spectators. They have taken spectators for granted and want them only to fork out in the form of lotteries, sponsorship, private boxes, (extortionately priced and enjoyed by a few people), and the only people who benefit from the game in so many ways, are the directors, the chairmen and the administrators. The two sets of people who are ignored and treated with scant consideration are the players and the spectators. If football clubs were developed on the lines of multi-sports complexes grounds could be used seven days a week. The revenue brought in would be colossal. There could be various forms of membership whether on a football basis, in the form of a season ticket or full membership, to enjoy squash, tennis, badminton, sauna baths, solariums and everything else that goes with multi-sports complexes. Having enrolled people a club would draw up a set of rules, especially for the football spectators, taking out membership cards, so if there were any abuse of the privileges implemented on their behalf the cards would be withdrawn. This should prevent any troublemakers from coming to a ground. If a troublemaker or a person misbehaves or is unruly at a private golf club, or a private tennis club or squash club, then that troublemaker is rooted out and his membership is not renewed, so one cuts out the root cause of the trouble and prevents it from happening again. The same sort of stringent rule would be applied to football centres. Hooliganism would then disappear. Cynics might say it sounds too simple. It is. Hooliganism does not occur at private clubs, except where a few members may get out of hand and then, as a result, forfeit their membership.

Clubs argue that there is no such thing as soccer-hooliganism, only hooliganism; that when it occurs in cinemas or public houses, no one talks about 'cinema hooliganism' or 'pub hooligans'. There is some reasoning in this. The hooligans make football an occasion for their misbehaviour. Football is not the cause of it. But we must face the problem and tackle it where it exists – and it *does* exist in and around some football grounds. Most clubs take the view that it can only be dealt with by the forces of law and order, that the initiative should come from the Home Office, the police and the law courts. But one does not have to accept responsibility to contribute to a cure. Football clubs are not responsible for hooliganism, but they *do* have a responsibility towards the safety of their genuine supporters and they can help to tackle hooliganism and its social causes by being more attentive to the recreational needs of the public. Instead of building metaphorical moats around their grounds, directors and managers should lower the drawbridges and bring themselves closer to people. Greater unity between club and public would help to diminish hooliganism, which rushes in to fill a vacuum. As I was writing this book I came across the following quotation:

'Our youth now have luxury. They have bad manners, contempt for authority. They contradict their parents, chatter before company, gobble up their food and tyrannise their teachers.'

This might sum up for many adults the attitudes of the modern younger generation. 'We were never like that,' is a well worn phrase. It might interest such people to know that the above passage was written by the philosopher, Plato, in the 4th century, BC. We ought to remember that when we were young, a few destructive and disrespectful youths gave our generation a bad name. 'Twas always so. The sins of one generation are visited on another.

There was an excellent chance twenty years ago for an example to be set on a national scale. The FA could have bought Wembley stadium for little more than £1 million. I was told this by the late Len Went, the stadium's Press officer. The Chester Committee recognised that it was out of date and ought to be modernised by the FA. A marvellous opportunity to acquire it at a bargain price and re-develop it, was thrown away. To paraphrase the hymn sung at Wembley before FA Cup finals, waste and decay in all around I see, FA the helpless, don't abide with me!

I have often wondered if there was some confusion about the Chester Report, whether the football authorities thought the Government should act on them and whether the Government thought the football authorities should take the initiative.

Successive governments have held the view that of the 36 principal recommendations of the Chester Report, the large majority were for the various football authorities to act upon and only three were for government action, namely those dealing with copyright in League fixture lists, taxation and the proposed football levy board.

The Commission on Industrial Relations report in 1974,

noted that in general the PFA supported most of the Chester Committee's proposals while the Football League and the FA were strongly critical of many of them. The League's view was that many of the Chester recommendations, especially those concerned with the transfer system, were impractical and if adopted could damage professional football in Britain. How wrong they were, we have seen in the strain imposed on clubs by excessive transfer fees. The PFA's grading system has been completely vindicated.

The Chester Report said that the transfer system, whereby one club may demand the payment of a fee from another club which desires to sign on one of its professional players, is deeply rooted in football, but is very rare in other professional occupations. The committee could appreciate the value to a club and to a player, of having professional players in formal contractual relationship with their clubs. 'But a contract which is renewable indefinitely on a year-to-year basis at the option of one of the parties seems to us to go beyond the normal contractual relationship and to be more one-sided than the situation demands.' In general, the Chester Committee was against one-way options, unless freely negotiated. It recommended that every contract between club and player should be for a definite period at the end of which either party should be free to renew it. A club afraid of losing a player would bargain for a longish period, say four, five or seven years. A player keen on security would bargain similarly. At the end of the agreed period, both parties being entirely free, the contract would be renewed for a further period by mutual consent. But neither the player nor the club would be under any legal obligation to renew. If the contract were not renewed, whether at the club's instance or at the player's, the player would not require the permission of his club to sign for another club. At the end of his contract a player would not be the property of his club. This is the rub.

The Chester Committee sought 'a moral basis' for the transfer system. It was from this base that the PFA conducted negotiations with the football authorities, for more than three years, trying to establish freedom of contract. Clubs can still retain a player's registration after his contract and the shackles are still there, loosened but not freed.

The Chester Report did not think it good for the game for

transfer fees to continue to rise and suggested a top level of £175,000 to £200,000. Looking back, how right they were! This seems small in the light of modern transfer fees, but how realistic and practical it would have been. High fees, said the committee, not only place a heavy responsibility on a highly priced player, but bewilder the general public and do harm to the image of the game, giving an impression that clubs have money to burn.

The money has been burned all right! Fortunes have been squandered that could have been spent on developing grounds as multi-purpose sports centres and on providing better social amenities for families.

Originally, Saturday afternoon football, watched from primitive spectator facilities, was an entertainment geared to an essentially working class audience, as the report observed back in 1968. Many spectators finished work at lunch time on Saturdays and then went to watch the local football team. Since then the work, leisure and family behaviour patterns of society have changed. Sports participation has increased, watching sport has declined. In the larger towns the potential spectators are now more scattered, living in the newly built suburbs and housing estates away from town centres. The five-day week has given families greater leisure and cars have given them more mobility. If there are a number of League clubs in an area, they are freer to patronise the most successful and the more attractive playing side.

Sport used to differentiate the classes. The working class was addicted to artisan sports, such as soccer, fishing, pigeon-racing, greyhound-racing and darts, while the middle and upper classes devoted their leisure time to the arts and the theatre. There are no social dividing lines today. Football itself has been 'intellectualised' by academically-minded university graduates, who have turned it into the art, for critical appraisal. But no matter how much modern football is analysed and discussed academically, it remains the common enjoyment of millions who simply want to be thrilled and entertained by what they see. The difference between 'then' and 'now' is that in the old days people did not expect football clubs to be any different to the backstreet areas where they were built. They accepted indifferent standards of comfort as they did in their own terraced homes.

Standards of cleanliness and comfort in the house – and the expectations of them outside – have risen. Many British football stadiums were built generations ago, when standards of comfort were much below what they are today. The bulk of accommodation is still for standing – a large part in the open, hardly ideal for a winter game. Refreshment and toilet facilities have fallen behind rising standards. Only a few clubs have possessed the money needed to provide satisfactory modern facilities.

A national opinion poll showed that a high proportion of football supporters gave cold and wet weather and lack of seating, covered stands and good toilet facilities as their main reason for not attending more often.

The range of leisure opportunities with which football must compete for people's spare time has expanded. TV especially has made a major, though complex, impact. It offers the public great quantities of sport in the comfort of their own homes.

All this was self-evident to the Chester Report, but continues to evade the football authorities. True, some clubs, such as Wolves, have built impressive new stands. But alas, the social facilities rarely match the stands themselves. A bright new stand is one thing; entertainment on the pitch and amenities behind or below the stands, are another.

Many new stands are only white elephants, built to further the misplaced ambitions of boards of directors, with little or no sense of priority, vision or foresight.

A club gets itself deep into overdraft with a bank to build a new stand, then finds it cannot afford to buy the players it needs to develop a successful side. The upshot is that the fans, unimpressed by what they see on the pitch, stay away. Success on the pitch should pave the way for re-development of the stands. And when they build new stands, they should include them in sports complexes, not hive off a large section of the space beneath and behind for private commercial use. As Gertrude Stein might have said, a seat is a seat is a seat.... What is the good of a seat in an expensive new stand if that is all it is? What is the essential difference between being seated in an 'old cowshed' and a new stand? One seat may have been wooden, the new one plastic. On his way to the new seat a spectator should be able to enjoy all manner of facilities and diversions.

The only people remaining in a football stadium after a

Saturday game are those in the £5,000- to £10,000-a-year glass-fronted boxes, helping themselves to drinks. They are insulated from the reality of a ground. Like directors, they are the privileged few, for whom football is an accessory for the Saturday afternoon entertainment; the directors and guests of successful companies, remote from ordinary spectators, who, in my opinion, are discouraged from regular and committed support by a system operating against their true interests. If present trends continue, there will come a time when the glass-fronted supporters, socialising as they watch, will be the only ones left!

Some clubs refuse to allow supporters' clubs to function, because they fear members will try to 'interfere' with the business of running the clubs. They don't want them 'poking their noses in' and there are clubs content to allow supporters to raise money for them but offer them nothing in return. Relationships between clubs and supporters, with one or two exceptions, are lamentable. I have known a club in the First Division, with a public relations expert and a commercial manager, to organise an open day for fans, with the promise of their being able to talk to players and get their autographs, then charge admission, only for the fans to find none of the players and only the assistant manager there to greet them.

No wonder supporters become soured and disillusioned, no wonder they drift away. If they are not made welcome, not made to feel that their support is important and are treated like stray cattle, they will lose pride in their clubs; they will turn to other interests.

It is sad that my old club, Wolves, has failed to recharge the batteries of supporters who in the fifties were among the most committed and passionate in the country. Molineux was often bursting at the seams. Now attendances have slumped. The new stand has not compensated for the disappointments of seasons without consistency and success. A couple of League Cup wins are not enough to engender the kind of support that marked the Stan Cullis period. In those golden days anyone in Wolverhampton who said in public that Wolves were rubbish, would have risked a punch on the nose. Now, anyone making a critical remark finds others agreeing with him. The club has not been developed to fit in with modern times and performances on the pitch have been below par. Consequently, the average attendance has slumped to around 20,000.

If a club like Liverpool or Manchester United can no longer guarantee regular gates of 50,000 plus, how can the likes of Wolves, Middlesbrough, Leicester City and the rest of them hope to break even and survive through gate receipts?

A feasibility study in 1978, on behalf of Ipswich Town FC to investigate furthering the club's financial potential, observed that football was in the red to the tune of £16 million* and 'the game will remain in this parlous state until each and every club takes a more commercial view of its activities'.

The irony is that clubs know what should be done. It would be extraordinary if they were not aware of what should be done, considering all the reports that have dropped on to the desks of directors and managers in recent years. Even the most cursory glance could enlighten them.

The Ipswich report by Marketing Solutions Ltd, of Salisbury Rd, Queens Park, London, referred to clubs in Germany, where there are no 'football' clubs as such. The game in Germany is organised at a local level by sports clubs, which also provide facilities for other sports, such as tennis, squash, basketball and volley-ball. Where professional football teams exist they represent the professional section of otherwise amateur clubs.

'It must be apparent even to the most casual observer that football has to compete for disposable income on far less favourable terms than a decade ago,' states the Ipswich report. 'Men and women tend to conduct their social activities much more together than previously; other sports are promoted more aggressively than football, usually due to their sponsorship by commercial organisations. Facilities at football grounds have not improved in line with increased quality demands by the consumer.'

In a summary of its findings, the report listed general bad management among the main reasons for the decline of English football. Unless there were a general tightening up of standards and facilities at grounds, it was unlikely that gates would increase. People interviewed mentioned exploitation of the public in excessive charges among the reasons for their loss of support.

* now over £20 million.

Some said, 'Wouldn't take a child there,' 'No longer a family game,' 'Not enough money put back into the game,' 'Pools firms are keeping too much money.'

When asked what single factors kept them away, six per cent said poor facilities and twelve per cent alternative pastimes. These comments were made mainly by men with young children. About thirty per cent said they would be prepared to pay more to watch their local side, but in return required a better deal. To them, this meant better facilities and better play on the pitch.

Referring to the CIR report four years earlier, the Ipswich study quoted a section of it: 'Structural reforms in the League have long been advocated but internal controversy has prevented radical change, Britain is not alone. . . . Throughout Europe clubs are having to come to terms with a new social environment in which rising living standards, increased mobility and the improvement of leisure facilities of all kinds, have given the public more choice in how to use their free time.'

The Ipswich report then made a damning comment: 'Nothing has changed since these words were written . . . If anything, we have seen an exacerbation of the problems facing football: increased hooliganism, the growing threat of "poaching" of the game's better players and managers by the North American League, the more sophisticated promotion of other sports and leisure activities and above all, the basic insolvency of the game. Football, in short, is in a mess. And much of that mess stems from poor management and direction and the failure to run football clubs on a sound commercial basis.'

The investigating team recommended building and developing sporting facilities in a sports complex, in partnership with the Sports Council and the local authority, taking as a model Crystal Palace or the Sobell Centre. I am not sure I would agree with these two examples as they appear to me to fall short in their aims and objectives.

'With continued high unemployment and the strong possibility of a shorter working week and early retirement, there can be no doubt that participation in sport and recreation are going to be of far greater significance in the next few years. Already we have the problem of the inner city kid and the coloured teenager. In some places 60 per cent of them are out of work, and they are sometimes delinquent because they have failed in life. Now if only they can find themselves through sport, whether by becoming good javelin throwers or skateboarders then they can hold their heads up. This is terribly, terribly important....'

The report suggested the development of small sites at comparatively small cost, into kickabout areas or ball parks, along with a plan to improve and upgrade facilities available at Portman Road, making them more generally available to a much more broadly-based club membership.

This, as I read it, would have been piece-meal and done in bits and pieces, when what is needed is a complete overhaul of a club and a new approach, backed with higher concepts of what a football club means in modern life.

Even so, the ideas were planted. Every director and manager in the League must by now have got wind of this kind of thinking. And still nothing happens. Lip service is paid to what should be provided and too little, or nothing at all, is provided for the public. Clubs are run the way they have been run for generations. They share with the designers of the Titanic a conviction that come what may, they are unsinkable – and they are steaming fast towards the iceberg which will sink them permanently unless they change course.

Here and there are encouraging signs, attempts to try something new and give the paying public value for money. But overall, the picture is bleak. Faced with recurrent financial crises, clubs continue to behave like profligate plunderers, plundering in the end only themselves. They plead poverty, warn of impending bankruptcy and then persuade a bank to lend them a fortune to spend on a player who might not even fit into the side and for whom they might still be paying, on hire purchase, long after he has fulfilled his contract and moved on.

Steve Daley was bought from Wolves by Manchester City, where Malcolm Allison was committed to the proposition that big buys could bring success. The price tag was £1.5 million and yet my former colleague failed to fit into the City side and became increasingly demoralised at Maine Road, until Big Mal's successor, John Bond, reduced his market value to around £400,000.

A few seasons ago, Manchester United, under Tommy Docherty, tried to buy success and only bought the club a passage to the Second Division. It is like an economist pumping money into circulation, convinced that this policy can spread prosperity and security and refusing to accept the lessons of failure. Huge transfer fees are counter-productive. The PFA's proposals for dealing with the transfer market would have brought commonsense and fairness to the system. Directors and managers who opposed the suggestions now plead that sky-high transfer fees are ruining the game. This is just what the PFA told them years ago.

We see managers who know they do not have cash to spare, pursuing players they know they cannot afford, like swimmers with broken arms leaping into the deep water, because this appears to be expected of them. They have to convince supporters that they mean business and are striving for success by building a strong side. When they cannot get the players they seek, they have a ready-made excuse for failure. They can argue it is not their fault and that success would have come had they been able to buy particular players. Wolves tried for several months to buy Peter Reid from Bolton and in the end announced that they could not afford him. They must have known from the start of negotiations whether they had the money, so why go through the motions, arouse supporters' expectations and then disappoint everyone, and especially the player?

You may well ask: Where has all the money gone? Much of it has gone on players who did not fulfil expectations and were then sold at a fraction of the sums for which they were bought. Meanwhile, ground conditions continue to deteriorate. Few football grounds justify the term 'stadiums'. Most have hardly altered in 40 years. When a club, like Wolverhampton Wanderers, builds a costly stand as part of a long-term rebuilding project it can be stuck with an albatross around its neck. The Molineux albatross is a heavy building debt which gate receipts cannot clear.

Another habitual failing is the conviction that simply by building a new stand, and then increasing the prices of the seats, the missing crowds will return, *en masse*. The time to lavish money on new facilities is when success has been achieved on the pitch, when a resourceful side has been created and consolidated. As Bill Shankly was fond of saying, crowds will turn up to watch a successful, exciting side even if the pitch is a roped off section of a field. A super-stand will not, by itself, attract the crowds. A super-team will. When the cash is coming in at the turnstiles and through sponsorship, which comes more readily to a successful side than to a struggling one, new facilities complement success on the pitch, rather than act as a substitute for it.

If these lessons are learned, they are only learned the hard way. Having rejected proposals which would have served the financial interests of their clubs, directors and managers are now bemoaning the system which has priced most of them out of the higher reaches of the market. How are the mighty fallen, bringing hardships on themselves! Poor Derby County, unable a third of the way through the 1980–81 season to find even £50,000 (a trifling sum by modern standards) for Aston Villa's midfield player, Alex Cropley. Yet it is amazing that Derby County have been reputed to be paying Roy McFarland nearly £50,000 a year, through contractual agreements, when his appearances have been few and far between, and yet cannot afford the same amount on a transfer fee.

Faced with huge wage bills and interest on money borrowed from the banks to build new stands, which they cannot fill, clubs can no longer afford the players they need to strengthen their teams and attract more spectators. Part of the trouble is that managers are not trained for financial administration, but they are expected to wheel and deal and negotiate in hundreds of thousands of pounds or millions. In what other industry would a manager be given so much responsibility, without any special training whatever? It is all part of the madness affecting the football industry, stemming from the top where 'gentlemen amateurs' continue to impose antiquated values and self-destructive attitudes on the game.

Three

Anyone who writes a book puts himself on the line, to face critics and those who demand that every word be justified. When I had published my last book, Derek Dougan's Doog, covering my career at Wolves and chairmanship of the PFA, I was put on the spot by interviewers, commentators, sports reporters and many individuals, asking what I would do to put football right. Stan Cullis, the former Wolves manager, who was among three interviewers asked by Midlands BBC to grill me over the book, said 'that if I were so unhappy with the present set-up, what would I do to alter it?'

Questions, questions, questions ... Answers were required. I could have trotted out a few clichés and tried to pacify my interrogators by turning a few phrases and I could have excused myself by saying I was in no position to do anything. But my mind was activated. I lay awake at night pondering the questions I had been asked. Just what would I do? At times, I fantasised, imagining myself as a benevolent dictator, with powers to initiate any changes I considered necessary for the betterment of the game. The idea developed to write another book, under the title How Not to Run a Football Club, based on experiences at my former clubs and especially at Kettering Town. I looked at a number of so-called 'blueprints' churned out by the FA, the Football League and the Managers' and Secretaries' Association. They offered nothing really new, nothing that would or could revitalise the game from top to bottom. This made me more determined to go ahead with the book and to call it How Not to Run Football. There would have been no need to write it had the football authorities paid serious attention to the many practical reports on the game over the past fifteen years. If they had, it would have been against my principles to go against them. In fact, I would have been pleased *not* to write this book.

It is staggering and depressing that the FA and Football League have ignored such detailed reports as the PEP (Political & Economical Planning) followed by the Chester Report, the CIR Report and one by the previous Minister of Sport in the Labour Government, Denis Howell. The Minister's report was a White Paper, entitled a White Paper on Sport and Recreation. Then came another report called the Rothschild Report, which again was a government established committee to look into gambling in sport. Numerous enquiries have followed the Ibrox Park disaster of 1971. I am concerned about the inability and the lack of initiative, by the football authorities, who have failed to bring our football out of 19th-century thinking.

I do not claim originality in all my views, which I have contributed to various reports over the years. There is nothing radically new in what I propose to regenerate football. Here, for instance, is what John Morgan wrote in the Daily Express in November, 1973, 'Soccer, half a dozen clubs aside, is a poverty stricken sport still clinging to a life-style that pertained half a century ago, yet we still have the same excessive numbers of stadiums, unused except for one day a week. They should be replaced by municipally-owned sports centres, of use to all the community, and rented by those clubs who can still make soccer a viable proposition.'

A month later, as I mentioned in my book On the Spot, subtitled Football as a Profession (published in 1974) the Sports Council declared that wherever possible professional football clubs should be developed to provide recreational facilities for the community. 'The club would become a focus of sports activity every day of the week, and by this means could establish itself on a sounder financial basis, at the same time fulfilling a public service in which the local authority would almost certainly be interested.'

My own comment and that of Dr Percy Young, co-author of On the Spot, then was that English football clubs belong to the towns and cities whose names they carry. By their activities they make those towns and cities better known and their citizens benefit in many and different ways.

There has been time, in the seventies, to put football grounds and the game itself on the right course, but lethargy lingers, not one of the 92 League clubs has even made a start in redeveloping their grounds as sports centres; not one has responded in anything more than academic or theoretical interest. We are plagued by an old British custom of setting up committees to produce reports, whose recommendations become nine-day talking points and are then forgotten. It is as if a report itself is the required product, not what is recommended.

Many people believe I should be proferring my views as a manager. Time and again I have been urged to enter management and certainly I have had plenty of offers. To be involved in the game as a manager under the present system would mean condoning a system which I despise and have repeatedly attacked. I have had experience of playing under thirty managers during the last 25 years. A thousand managers have had the sack since the Second World War and not all of them have been bad managers. The system, at the end of their playing days, has not been able to equip them for managing football clubs.

People involved in the game confidently expected me to go into management when I ended my playing career. I decided in July of 1974, that I would retire at the end of the following season although I had two years of my contract remaining. I decided to retire for two reasons. Firstly, I could not continue any longer at the highest level of the First Division because of a back injury, which had been giving me spasmodic problems over 20 years. Secondly, I could not tolerate the inhospitable environment perpetuated over seven years at Wolverhampton Wanderers by the manager, Bill McGarry.

The playing climax of my career at Wolverhampton Wanderers came when we won the League Cup, beating Manchester City at Wembley, on 2 March 1974. It was on this occasion, after the match, when I was offered the position of player-manager of Aston Villa. The offer came from the club's chairman Doug Ellis, during a conversation at the Wolves' celebration banquet at the Hilton hotel. It was a flattering offer and I was gratified to think that my old club, where I had taken so much pride putting on the claret-and-blue shirt, wanted me to play again and to manage. But I had to be realistic. I knew that my recurrent back trouble, which had begun at Villa Park, would prevent my operating effectively in a dual capacity at that level of football. I had to be frank with Doug Ellis and tell him that I was not up to the task, physically, for the dual role.

We continued to talk, for quite a while. Then he suggested that if I did not feel able to join Aston Villa as player-manager, why not come simply as manager? A lot of thoughts raced through my head. What beautiful irony, I thought, if I returned to Villa Park as manager eleven years after a previous manager, Joe Mercer, had booted me out. There was no time, however, for fantasising. I had to make up my mind on the spot or ask for time to consider the invitation. Other thoughts began going through my mind. The Villa manager at the time was Vic Crowe, who had been one of my team-mates at Villa. It had been no secret in those days that we were not exactly chums. I sometimes wondered whether as team captain he kept the manager informed of what was said in the dressing room. It was only a suspicion, which may seem paranoiac, but I have always suspected that many team captains and trainers, who are closer to players during the week than most managers, bend an ear and 'keep managers posted'. All I knew for sure is that Joe Mercer seemed remarkably well informed. He did not have to be in the dressing room to know what was said. When Vic joined me at Peterborough I changed my mind about him and came to admire his professionalism and his attitude towards the game, at the same time I was revising my own attitudes.

When Doug Ellis put the proposition to me, at a time I was pondering my future career in football, I wondered what acceptance would mean to Vic and to his family. How would he feel if I negotiated for his job? It is true that football is a notoriously cut-throat profession and that often survival depends on looking after one's own interests, even at the expense of others. Plenty of managers have been known to shake hands when they meet at one another's grounds, while concealing the knives behind their backs. It would, I suppose, be asking too much for them to say: Hello, I'm after your job. I've been talking to the chairman about it.'

If Doug Ellis had terminated Vic Crowe's contract, I might have considered the offer. As it was, I speculated what might happen in a couple of years' time. Would someone else be offered the job behind my back? I told him I would think it over, but frankly my mind was already made up, on the spot.

I did not think I could take on Aston Villa on a daily business, in spite of my great affection for the club. I could not see myself in the position offered to me. In our conversation I doubted whether our temperaments were compatible. Other ideas were crystallising in my mind. I was thinking of different ways to further my footballing interests. Taking shape, in my imagination, was a football club (unspecified) as the basis of a multi-purpose sports centre when I had finished playing for Wolves. I looked around for a suitable club in need of transformation, and my gaze settled on Walsall FC, a few miles from my home.

Over the months my ideas fermented and a year later I requested a meeting with the chairman of Walsall Football Club, Mr Ken Weldon. On arrival at the ground I had a look around what can only be described as a relic of the 19th century. Clubs like Walsall are in such poor condition, one can only sympathise with the players and the spectators. A small hut turned out to be the boot room. There were a couple of young fellows cleaning boots, one of them the brother of Allan Clarke. I asked them the way to the main office. The secretary, John Westmancoat was expecting me and I was standing in his office when the manager, Duggie Fraser, came in. He looked at me and when I greeted him I felt slightly uncomfortable because I wanted to tell him why I was there but I couldn't because it was a confidential matter. I am sure he felt I was there to join them as a player or I was going to take over as manager. Before getting down to the business which had brought me to Fellows Park I was staggered when Ken Weldon told me: 'We tried to get you on loan, and we spoke to Bill McGarry.' I don't know who the 'We' were and I didn't ask him. I was incensed that McGarry should have entered into discussions about my going to Walsall on loan, or with the possibility of my joining them at the end of the season, because I had already told him the previous July that I was retiring. This incidentally, is one of the reasons I have been obsessed by campaigning for a better deal and for the entire contractual system to be changed for players. Managers (and mis-managers) feel that players are to be bought and sold at their discretion without the players' views even being sought.

When the meeting got underway, I said to Mr Weldon: 'I

have only one question to ask you, would you run your business like you run your football club?' He said, 'No.' I asked him why not. He shrugged his shoulders and said, 'Is there any other way?' I said, 'Yes.' I spoke for two hours about why I wanted to take over Walsall Football Club. When you have a strong interest in something you suddenly see what is needed. I knew what Walsall needed. I wanted to take over the club for a number of reasons. I had just moved house, and felt that I could live in that house for the rest of my days. My children were at schools where they could finish their education. I felt the time was right for football clubs to change their approach and I wanted to try to give them an insight into how a football club could and should be run.

Walsall seemed to offer the ideal challenge and opportunity. Here was a small, struggling club, rarely getting gates of more than 4,000. If I could take it over and successfully transform it into a community centre, with the football club as its mainstay, the way would be open for other clubs to emerge from the past into the late 20th century. I assured Mr Weldon that I had no animosity towards him or his directors, his manager or anyone else at the club. It happened, I explained, that I had come to see him with my proposition because I lived in the region and that if I had lived near to Watford or Wrexham, I would have made the same approach to them.

He asked me if I were alone in the proposed venture and I told him, 'Yes.' Towards the end of our conversation he asked me if I would be interested in managing the club. This bemused me, because it was not what we had been talking about. I said, 'Obviously, you didn't hear me right, Mr Weldon. I am interested only in taking over the club.' The upshot was that he would call a special board meeting and put my offer to the directors and then let me know their decision.

Two weeks passed without any contact. Then came a telephone call from Mr Weldon. He said, 'I've been instructed to give you this message: "You have no chance of taking over control of Walsall Football Club."'

I was disappointed, but not surprised. I said: 'Well, Ken, if you change your mind or have a change of heart, please let me know.' And that was that. I did not hear from the club again, until I made another, similar approach four years later, when once more my offer was turned down, only this time it did not get as far as a directors' meeting.

Unable to get a foot in the door at Fellows Park did not unsettle my plans. When my contract at Wolverhampton Wanderers ended I decided to spend three months away from it all and then make up my mind about the future. In the summer I was with Bobby Moore and Bob Wilson in Brazil for an indoor soccer tournament and we had a lot of time for exchanging ideas about the game. They agreed that my ideas were constructive, but they considered them revolutionary. I said, 'Not really, it's the only way ahead.' Perhaps if they had taken a more active interest in the PFA and had studied all the reports available on the game, they would not have been so conservative to describe my scheme as 'revolutionary'.

My disappointment over Walsall's reaction was short-lived. After the Fellows Park door had closed, another opened, which was a favourite saying of Dave Burnside, a team-mate at Wolves. 'In football,' he used to say, 'when one gate shuts, another one opens.'

Four

One day I had a telephone call from John Nash, chairman of Kettering Town Football Club, I said, 'What can I do for you?' and he said, 'I would like you to come and take over Kettering Town Football Club. Would you be interested?' I immediately said, on the telephone, 'Do you know exactly what taking over Kettering Town Football Club means, Mr Nash?' He said, 'Yes,' and I said, 'Well, what does it mean?' He said, 'Well, I want you to come and manage it,' and I said, 'No, I don't want to manage it, I want to run it.' He then said, 'What is the difference?' I said, 'It's very simple. A manager only manages, whereas I feel and I know what my experience tells me, that I want to run a football club.' But I went back to the takeover side of it and I said, 'Are you trying to say to me that you are offering to sell me this football club?' 'No,' he said, 'I want you to manage it.' I said I was not really interested in managing it, but I would be interested in running the club. We agreed to meet, and he came to my home, arriving in a Rolls-Royce. I wondered if he had borrowed it to create an impression or did he own it? It turned out that he owned it. The meeting at my house in Wolverhampton lasted for four hours, I left him in no doubt I wanted to run the club from top to bottom, the commercial development, the team, the financial side, and everything else that goes with running a football club in the latter part of the 20th century. Kettering was not too far from my home to prevent my commuting, by car. This encouraged me because I was anxious to stay in the Wolverhampton district and not disturb my two boys' education.

A few meetings were held to clarify the details we would encounter in my involvement with Kettering Town Football Club. I had everything translated into an official legal document, between my own company and Kettering Town Football Club. My agreement was drawn up by Mr George Davies the official solicitor of the Professional Footballers' Association. Mr Davies said he had never seen so much control in a football contract in his career in drawing up agreements. John Nash made it clear to me during our meetings that any issue, large or small, should not be discussed with other members of the board, but that he and I would decide what we should do.

Why did I go from the glamour of a First Division club and opt for the future development of a non-league club? Simply, I would be in control of my own destiny. What I didn't know at the time and it would take me eighteen months to find out, was the true extent of the financial problems at Kettering Town Football Club.

The excitement following my appointment was immense and the interest it created in and around Northampton was very high indeed. The first game I played, considering that the club had slumped to gates of 1,000 or so, there was more than 3,000. Fog though, was so bad when the game started, we could not play for more than 60 minutes. The directors were well pleased by its having to be abandoned. At first, I was puzzled. Then I was told that the spectators were not entitled to their money back and would have to pay again to see the match played again. The referee that night was something of a hero! The attendance produced a considerable amount of money for a non-League club. At that time I did not realise just how important cash was to the club.

The next two seasons were to bring me the greatest possible experience of How Not To Run A Football Club. John Nash to his credit never interfered in the running of the club. He left it entirely to me. I was looking forward to the opportunity of taking part in a board meeting. In my first book 'Attack' the first part of my autobiography, I described a conversation with the chairman of Leicester City, Len Shipman, when we were returning by train from a match. He asked what my ambitions were and I said my ambition was to sit as an invisible man and listen to what directors discussed about running a football club. I had to wait a long time to achieve it. Ten years after that conversation the day came. Directors of Kettering included Tom Bradley, a Labour MP, Terry Gray, an insurance broker, Fred Harlow, a doctor. The Board meetings didn't turn out as I envisaged.

The chairman and I did most of the talking. Len Parker said afterwards to me I was a 'breath of fresh air'. I said, 'What do you mean by that?' and he said, 'Well, normally in the past we only heard the chairman and very little comment about anything from the other directors. It seemed to me that it was just a one-man band where John Nash would open a meeting and chair everything while the other directors would agree with him. Mr Parker worked with him and he was a director of one of John Nash's companies. I soon had a feeling that if John Nash wasn't about or within earshot, everything would subsequently get to him.

This reminded me of my experiences at various clubs as a player. Time and again what were supposed to be confidential conversations in the dressing rooms would be carried to managers and directors, as if walls had ears or H. G. Wells's Invisible Man was there, listening in and taking notes. Incidentally, I found out later at Kettering which director reported all to the chairman.

I quickly noticed that Len Parker took and kept the minutes of board meetings, which seemed to me strange, as he was the financial director. But I did not query this at the time.

The secretary of the football club was Mr Maurice Marston, who I discovered had signed a ten-year contract as commercial manager. When I arrived he was no longer commercial manager. His title was club secretary. This confused me a little because I always thought that the secretary of a limited company, or of a football club, took the minutes of meetings and performed other secretarial duties. Maurice was admitted for one item on the agenda, correspondence. He had to sit outside the meetings, waiting to be invited in to give his report and go through the correspondence as it came in, from one board meeting to the next. I felt this must have been humiliating for him. I was instructed by the directors not to take any notice of him, regarding the club and on reflection, it was wrong of me to accept this instruction. It was seven or eight months before we had a meeting and matters were brought to a head. I must put on record that Maurice Marston was devoted to Kettering Town FC and gave me 100 per cent support during my tenure.

I did not realise that the club's finances were in such dire straits. The local bank manager knew, which is why he received a jolt when he read in the Press that I was being paid £15,000 a year salary by the club. When he phoned to find out what was going on he was put right. It was not the first time the Press had exaggerated matters involving me. I thought it would be a sensible idea to have words with the bank manager to discuss the financial situation of the club, but I learned it was dealt with at a higher level, in London, by someone named Mike Craker. Eventually, I discovered that the club had five bank accounts and had a system of borrowing from one account to pay into another, to spread the load.

The bank must accept some responsibility for allowing the club to get into such a financial mess. I did not have any money to spend on new players and it was a case of persisting with those we had, trying to turn them into a winning side. When I inquired into their state of fitness in preparation for the season, the players told me that they were by no means over-exerted in their preparatory training. To be fair, between December and the end of the season, they did not do too badly for me, though five or six players were certainly not good enough for the Southern League over the next season, if we were to fulfil our ambitions. I quickly took on former Wolves colleague, Brian Thompson, as my assistant and I left to him the training and coaching while I tried to re-organise the club's commercial activities. I was having to cope with all sorts of problems and difficulties and I did not realise they were so acute until my February pay cheque bounced at the bank.

I was astonished when it was sent back to me marked 'Refer to Drawer'. The club did not have enough funds to meet my salary. When another monthly pay cheque was returned to me from the bank I expressed my concern to Len Parker as financial director and he informed the chairman. There was no point in my re-submitting the cheque to the bank if there were insufficient funds in the account. This happened to me half a dozen times between February 1976 and August 1977.

The financial strain on the club was caused by lack of thought and consideration by those who should have sought more constructive advice. There had obviously been considerable maladministration in the recent past. I was now faced with it. One of my problems was the main stand, which I was told had cost £100,000. It must be the only football stand in the country with the directors' box at the end, instead of the middle. The trouble with the stand was the awkward staircases, which made me apprehensive for public safety when we had a good FA Cup run and were getting large attendances.

A lot of money, around £80,000, had been spent on a bowling green at the club, but this had been closed through lack of public support before I arrived. I had to take things as I found them and begin from there. I soon discovered that a balance sheet does not always reveal the true extent of affairs.

My contract was a modest one, £600 a month and I was on 50 per cent of all commercial ventures I could introduce to the Club. Sponsorship seemed to me the best way of introducing money into the club for two reasons. It would be simple to operate and it was an ideal way for a local firm or a big company to give money to a football club. Their investment would yield a lot in publicity and exposure. I looked around and I happened to notice one night on television an advertisement for Kettering Tyres, who were based at Wellingborough and after a couple of meetings with their directors I was sweating on the outcome. They said that they would get in touch, I had a feeling that it was going well. The one question they didn't ask me in these talks was the involvement of Kettering Tyres with Kettering Town. Would it sell an extra set of tyres? I had the answer ready for them and the answer was 'I don't know about selling any extra set of tyres but what I *do* know is that you spend an awful lot of money promoting your product "Kettering Tyres" and all the other accessories that go with your business. I will get you a lot of exposure in the newspapers. You will be on the radio, spoken about and shown on television.'

Exhibiting a scrapbook, I said to them, 'Not only will I get you one of these full, I will get you two filled.' I was true to my word, although I must admit that the publicity came overwhelmingly out of an unforeseen conflict between Kettering Town FC and the football authorities. The exposure the company received for a modest investment of £2,500 was incredible. Day after day, week after week, 'the KT affair' loomed large in newspapers, on radio and on television. In some instances it was presented as a battle between me and the football hierarchy. If so, it was not a confrontation of my seeking. My only interest was in promoting Kettering Town FC and initiating a money-raising scheme, which I knew would pave the way for other clubs. Looking back on the issue, it is hard to understand all the fuss. Sponsorships have become commonplace, coming from individuals, small and large companies and big conglomerates, who feel they are justified in ploughing money into sport, from grass roots to the top. All manner of teams in amateur football have sponsors' names on their jerseys and now it is accepted for League clubs to advertise their sponsors, on shirts and tracksuits – and rightly so, because football has to survive and if it cannot find the means to flourish at the lowest level, we shall not have the Keegans, the Shiltons, the Jennings, Bests and Charltons coming through.

When I began sponsorship negotiations on behalf of Kettering Town, I did not anticipate the furore it was to cause among FA officials. The first indication that something was amiss came when I received a letter from the FA informing me that I was in breach of the rules and must not wear a sponsor's name on our shirts. I took no notice of this because, looking at the FA rulebook at that time, I could find no reference to an actual instruction that a player could not wear such a shirt. Over the next few months I exchanged letters on the subject with the FA and we continued to wear the shirts. All this time the club and Kettering Tyres were becoming household names, thanks to the Press publicity. Matters came to the boil when an official of a non-League club informed the FA that we had worn the shirts in a match against his team.

At the next board meeting I could hardly restrain my excitement. I had clinched a £2,500 sponsorship deal which meant that the ten home games remaining before the end of the season worked out at £250 a game. As chief executive, I was gratified to be able to report such a successful commercial move on behalf of the club. Not long afterwards I happened to meet the Norwich manager, John Bond, at a hotel near to Coventry, and we chatted about sponsorship. He was delighted over a sponsorship deal of £500 for Norwich's home match against Liverpool. To think that little Kettering, in the Southern League, was getting half of the amount a first division club had negotiated, was greatly heartening for me. But the thought struck me that here was a respected First Division manager having to give his time and attention to a commercial project which should have been the concern of the commercial manager. All his thoughts should have been on the actual game against Liverpool. Too many managers are involved in matters that should not divert their attention from team affairs.

The euphoria over Kettering Tyres' sponsorship was increased by knowledge that we would be pioneering something which other clubs had only talked about. No one could deny that Kettering Town needed the money, after the failure of other commercial schemes. For instance, the club had started a Cash and Carry business and had signed a long lease, with rent of £6,000 a year paid in quarterly instalments. The venture had gone badly wrong and the business had been closed before I arrived on the scene.

When Mr Len Parker said of the sponsorship deal, 'Oh, now we can pay Fairbond,' I thought he was referring to an outstanding debt involving one of the former players. It turned out that Fairbond was the name of the Cash and Carry company.

Money – or the lack of it – was on everyone's mind. The more I thought of it, the more obvious it was that sponsorhip was the short-term answer to the club's financial problems.

I knew how sports in other countries had benefited from sponsorship schemes, while deep-seated puritanism and suspicion had prevented similar schemes being embraced in Britain. Diehards were still insisting that commerce and sport should not mix, that if sport became dependent on commercial involvements it would lose its independence. My own view was that if it remained aloof and tried to 'go it alone' it would lose more than its independence. It would lose its lifeblood. Commercial backing did not mean a football club surrendering itself to outside interests, any more than a theatre encouraging sponsorship schemes would be affected in its productions or administration. It seemed to be good sense to attract sponsors, thereby guaranteeing funds when the turnstiles cannot click enough to wipe out overdrafts and debts.

The deal I worked out with Kettering Tyres ensured that players would not become running sandwichboard men on the pitch. Everything was planned tastefully and discreetly. There was no vulgarity, no razmataz to overwhelm the normal activities of the ground. But I did not anticipate the angry reaction of the Football Association, which was to bring its big guns to bear as if I had struck at the foundations of its rules and regulations.

Although there was no specific rule binding me, for the sake of discretion I had another shirt made, with a beautiful KT on the left side to signify the club and the sponsor. The football authorities, however, were not to be swayed. The day of reckoning came in May 1976, the day before the FA Cup Final. I reported to the Football Association with the club chairman, who was not happy about having to go in front of them. He had been on holiday when Tom Bradley and I went to the first hearing, before an FA committee, which decided that they wanted the chairman to be present and postponed the hearing. This was reported in the Press in such a way that John Nash had the feeling he was being summoned before them like an errant schoolboy ordered to report to the headmaster's study for a ticking off. He was slightly angry and apprehensive, being unsure what to expect.

Having appeared before many disciplinary hearings and countless meetings on behalf of the PFA, I had a good idea what to expect, but I did not anticipate that they would field their 'international team' against us. I expected there would be one or two high ranking officials present. Instead, they had Sir Harold Thompson, who is now the FA chairman; Bob Lord, the outspoken and volatile chairman of Burnley FC; Vernon Stokes, who presided over disciplinary hearings involving players alleged to have committed misdemeanours on the pitch; the former chairman of the FA, the late Sir Andrew Stephen; Mr A. D. Mullen (now vice-chairman), and Ted Croker, Secretary of the FA. It was a formidable line-up.

John Nash and I gave a fair account of ourselves. The FA had not seen the players in the 'offending' strip, so I could afford to give them a bit of waffle. I said that we no longer wore the strip bearing the name of Kettering Town FC. I had introduced the initials KT and I had had made a couple of other attractive designs, with the emblem. These I kept up my sleeve, well, not literally up my sleeve, but in my briefcase to display during the meeting. On behalf of the club, I claimed ignorance of any rule and I still maintain that the rule book of 1972 did not specify that a sponsor's name could not be worn on a shirt. If the FA council had decided against it at one of its meetings, it failed to enter the new rule in the FA rule book.

We had played in the jerseys for more than dozen games, but I admitted to having used them a few times. Then I showed them the jersey bearing the initials KT. One of the committee members said, 'Well, you are still wearing the name, even with the KT, this is against the rules,' which I contend, was not. They had to admit that KT could have stood only for Kettering Town, but in their minds it was all tied up with a tyre company. What angered me was that here were the top people in the FA unable or unwilling to grasp the fact that little clubs had to help themselves. They did not understand that they as leaders of a big 'international club' ought to assist, not hinder, the small fry who belonged to it. I was taken aback by the gravity of Vernon Stokes (a former director of my old club, Portsmouth), when he tried to impress on me the seriousness of my offence. He said, 'Do you know we could close down your ground?' This struck me as odd because it was not my ground. I thought he was giving me a lot of twaddle. He repeated the warning and added, 'If you continue to wear the name on the particular jersey.' As he droned on I began to day-dream and finally I had to shrug myself back to reality.

There was really no need, I thought, for him to go to that length. The football hierarchy believes it has absolute power, though I must add that Ted Croker, the present FA secretary, was fair, polite and considerate. The committee rumbled on, with the exception of Mr Mullen, who was courteous and polite and who, on other occasions when I was present, never had much to say.

It saddens me to this day that the football authorities did not take the trouble to come to Kettering to see for themselves what we were trying to do in our sponsorship scheme and how discreet we made the advertising on jerseys. If they had done so, they might have taken a more understanding attitude.

Their attitude set my mind thinking about a lot of issues and to recap as having described in the past an FA disciplinary hearing as, on the one hand having a bed of nails and a bucket of whitewash on the other, I have also gone on record as saying that if the FA or the Football League could horse-whip a player in public, or possibly get away with hanging one of us, they would do so because some of them are convinced that the ills of the world today and certainly of the UK, stem from professional footballers. This attitude is still prevalent today. Players and legislators are often light years apart. I recall one top administrator saying he would not hang a dog on the word of a footballer and a director of a top club saying that a footballer could not run a fish and chips shop, to which my answer was that I knew plenty of players who could run fish and chips shops, but not many directors. At a meeting between the PFA and the games administrators, Bob Lord, the chairman of Burnley FC, turned to me at one point and said, 'Dougan, why don't you leave the administration to us and get on with playing the game?' I wonder if he would care to repeat that question, now that Burnley are in the Third Division!

Going back to my appearance in front of the Football Association, it brought a great deal of interest. Reporters and photographers were waiting for me in the corridor. After an hour Mr Nash and I were sent out of the room. We had to stand outside which seemed humiliating, like troublesome schoolboys waiting outside the headmaster's study while their punishment is decided. There was no anteroom where we could sit. The Press asked me, 'How did it go?' and I said, 'Well, it went as expected,' and I said, 'Obviously, gentlemen, I cannot influence the outcome, but I know what the outcome is going to be.' This surprised John Nash, because he felt that we were going to be fined £1,000. This was the figure that he had put on it. He said we would also be seriously censored. I said to him, 'I don't have my crystal ball, but I will tell you what the outcome is going to be, we are going to be brought back in there, they are going to look at you and I, Mr Chairman (I had fallen into the habit of addressing him as Mr Chairman at times) and they are going to say, 'You have behaved like a couple of naughty boys, irresponsible, you have flaunted the FA Rules, and this time we are going to let you off with a severe warning.' If you can imagine the scenario standing like a couple of kids before the headmaster, in view of the entire school, and you can picture the headmaster finger wagging and telling everybody how naughty we were before letting us off with a reprimand, I went on to say, 'Mr Chairman, we will get away with a stern warning, and no fine at all. The only thing we will have to pay is our expenses coming down to London.' He said, 'You must be kidding. They have been to all this trouble, they must fine us to save face.' I said, 'I know these people, there is nothing that they can possibly do because we haven't broken the rules, they know it and I know it, and we will get away with a warning.' The PFA under my chairmanship had often taken on the Establishment and won and I saw no reason for any qualms on this occasion, even if a lot of hot air would blow our way.

We were called back into the room, and Sir Andrew Stephen said that they had considered all the facts in this particular case, which I thought was laughable, because they had never even been to a ground to see us wearing the strip. I felt like correcting him saying that they had considered all the 'hearsay'. Vernon Stokes chipped in, saying, 'If this ever happens again, we will close your ground down indefinitely, but we are letting you off as long as you promise to give your word that you will not do it again,' John Nash assured them we would not wear the names of the sponsor on the jerseys again, and I admired him for this. But at the same time it riled me to hear it. He should not have felt obliged to kow-tow when we had acted solely in the interest of the football club.

I realised the following day, while watching the Cup Final on TV why we had been let off so leniently, when they had self-given powers to invoke heavy penalties. It all fell into place in the close-ups of players sporting sponsors' emblems, logos, advertisements *et al* on behalf of the Football Association! Oh, yes, they allowed the Southampton and Manchester United teams to wear the unmistakable identification of Admiral, which had a commercial contract yielding a lot of money for the FA. And yet they were against little Kettering Town trying to look after itself in a similar way.

These double standards in football enrage me. I am in favour of anyone getting as much out of sponsorship as they can, on behalf of their clubs and I am against anyone trying to prevent others from pursuing this legitimate cause.

It's an ill wind ... The extra exposure that came from the dispute with the FA made it a lot easier for me to re-negotiate a better deal with Kettering Tyres for the following season, almost three times what we had previously received. Furthermore, the Press, for the first time, were united for me against the soccer Establishment. I believe it was the first time they were united on my behalf.

As chief executive of Kettering Town, I was being pulled in different directions at the same time, trying to promote the club's commercial interests and making efforts to strengthen the team and improve our League position. The sponsorship issue demanded a great deal of my time and energy, but I was careful not to neglect the all-important business of what happened on the pitch, at home and away. At times, journeying back and forth, between my home in Wolverhampton and Northants, I felt emotionally close to exhaustion, but I was stimulated by the challenge and excited by the ideas I hoped to bring to fruition. I had succeeded in getting this little club talked about throughout the country. At the same time I knew the perils of running a club that was only 'talked about'. It had to prove itself and could only do that on the pitch. I realised by the end of the 1975–76 season that the first team was not good enough. So I set about getting together a squad of players 'on the cheap'. There are plenty of footballers in and around non-League football with immense, but undiscovered skill and talent. Having no money to spend did not mean we had to be short of quality players. My signings did not cost me anything, not even Terry Mortimer (reminiscent of Bruce Rioch and in my judgment a better player). Dunstable wanted £200 for him, representing the ten weeks' wages they had paid to him while was recovering, after an ear operation. I thought this was a mean demand and I was not impressed by their way of doing business. I did not see why we should pay back to them the wages they had paid him under contract, but this was a condition they laid down. I decided that a little subterfuge was needed. When I arranged for the two clubs to play a friendly fixture at Kettering and split the proceeds, I told Maurice Marston to lob as many expenses as possible, so in the event we finished by getting the player without having to pay Dunstable anything.

Before the start of the 1976–77 season, all the Kettering players were rarin' to go. They had their hearts in their training and responded well in pre-season to all the hard work prepared for them by me, and my assistant Brian Thompson. They also responded eagerly when a friend, Freddie McFaul, suggested that we take a team to Northern Ireland for a few pre-season matches. He arranged for us to play Crusaders, Coleraine, Glenavon and Carrickfergus. We won three of the games and our team spirit, stimulated in those eight days on tour, was so strong that we went on to remain unbeaten in the League until New Year's Day, 1977, when we were still involved in five competitions.

But even the most successful and ambitious side cannot legislate or guard against bad luck and we had our share of it at a crucial time. A blow to the first team came when Mike Wardrop broke his leg, a setback which eventually finished his career at that level. He was a young player of tremendous ability. He could hold the ball, shake off defenders and provide that little extra which turns an ordinary team into a good one. His injury presented me with acute problems on the right side of the pitch, so I decided to adopt a four-two-four formation. There were occasions when we would have been more effective with a four-three-three line-up, to counter opponents bent on defensive tactics. Not that I have absolute faith in formations, which are often applied too rigidly at the expense of an intuitive response to what happens in a game. The trouble with formations is that they cannot take into account the unexpected – and football is a game of the unexpected. At non-League level I would say that exceptional fitness can be decisive in winning matches, which is why I emphasised it at the start of a season. What happened in training, I said, would have a strong bearing on our League position at the end of the season. When Mike Wardrop was out of the squad, I knew we were one player short of having a team capable of winning the Southern League championship, which was won by Wimbledon.

My next stroke of ill fortune involved the goalkeeper, Gordon Livesey. For some months he had off-the-pitch problems. They were so bad they would have demoralised anyone with less resilience. It amazed me that with so many off-the-field distractions he was able to concentrate on his game. When on New Year's Day we lost four – one to Margate, I put it down as a momentary lapse and I made no move to replace Gordon in goal. I regarded him as my most consistent player and I certainly was not going to desert him because he had personal problems threatening to weigh him down. But a month later, when we had been beaten by Colchester and we were out of all Cup competitions, it was obvious that his difficulties had got the better, or the worst, of him and I was forced, reluctantly, to leave him out of the team. Staying in the Cup competitions was important, not just for players' prestige and morale, but to ease the club's financial predicament.

Everyone in the Southern League and around the local area imagined that Kettering Town was a wealthy club because of the chairman's own position as a reputed millionaire involved with many companies. After I had discovered the parlous state of the club, it seemed to me that the best way to get the club on a strong and healthy financial footing was for me to acquire it and with this aim in mind, after the resignation of the chairman on 18 May 1977, I entered into negotiations with the Midland Bank in London. The bank's financial director, Mike Craker, told me that John Nash had asked the bank to take over the club to clear outstanding debts, but the suggestion had been turned down. Other directors had believed what they were told by Mr Nash about the possibility of the bank taking over control. I decided there was no point at this stage in discussing with them what I had in mind, until there was a definite move in favour of my plan. Numerous meetings were held and I tried in vain to determine the full extent of the chairman's financial involvement, so I would know what he might lose should the club be put into liquidation. He stressed when he resigned as chairman that he would not leave the club in any sort of financial predicament.

When Mike Craker came to see me in Kettering he told me they could scarcely believe in London how I had kept the club going from December 1975, until my meeting with him – and I was consoled by his remark. But it became clear to me, if not to the directors, that the bank was not interested in acquiring the club and it would have to work out its own salvation.

I stopped drawing players' wages, because there was no money in the account to pay them. None of the directors raised the matter. Nor did they ask how the wages were to be paid. I sometimes had to fall back on a ruse, sending the secretary home and then telling the players that he had flu and would not be able to hand out their pay packets until the weekend.

We would wait for the lottery money to be collected on Friday, and use this to pay the wages on Saturday.

Eventually, I went to see the new chairman, Tom Bradley, to go with him through the whole financial position of the club. He gave me the impression that he was astonished and flabbergasted by all I told him. I explained that I had established a reasonable financial structure for the rest of the season, but if I could not assume control of the club to run it as a sports complex, then I did not want to spend the next three years struggling financially.

Tom Bradley was the only director I asked to do anything for me. As he was an MP I asked him to arrange a meeting with Denis Howell, the Minister of Sport, to expound on the ideas advanced in his White Paper on Sport. Almost two years later I was still waiting for the meeting to be arranged.

For two seasons I had strained to get the club out of its financial doldrums. In the circumstances, it might have seemed reckless to propose going ahead with transforming the club into a sports complex, but I felt a long-term view had to be taken, to give the club something to aim for and to involve the public. Support for the club, I reckoned, would increase all over the Northants region if it became the base of a sports community centre, serving as a nucleus of social and recreational life in the community. The groundwork required long and patient negotiations with the town council and the Sports Council. But before the scheme could get underway, we had to test public opinion. An appeal for initial funds, to start the first phase, met with encouraging response in some quarters but negative response in others. I came to the conclusion that the people of Kettering could not believe their luck; they had been so used to living in a town where big, important recreational schemes did not happen, they remained suspicious and sceptical, as if it were too good to happen to them. And so the appeal failed to meet its target and the scheme fell through at the very moment the club had an unprecedented opportunity to rid itself of the mistakes of the past and prepare itself for new concepts in the future.

Sadly, I find that little has changed since I left. On 18 November 1980, I read in the Kettering Evening Telegraph that Terry Rose had quit his post as general manager after six months as money raising supremo, following what was described as 'the rapid deterioration of relationships with his employers'.

He said he was 'promised things', but the most he took home was £47. Before flying to South Africa to start a new venture in the motor industry, he said Kettering were the best non-League club in the business but needed stronger leadership. 'You've only got to look at the financial history of the club to see there's been something wrong a hell of a long time. It needs rearranging completely and I think I disturbed a bit of a hornet's nest when I arrived.' He was annoyed by the lack of recognition for the Supporters' Association. 'They and the fans are taken for granted,' he said, reflecting my own feelings about many League and non-League clubs.

Tom Bradley, the chairman, said that nearly all the cash raised by the sale of players since May 1980, about £12,000, had gone to keep the club alive. 'If it hadn't been for money received from transfer fees we could not have survived,' he admitted. What a damning statement, what an indictment of a system common throughout football. In other words, a club's most valuable assets, players, have to be sold to keep the club going – and for how long? What happens when there are no players to be sold? What happens when the playing strength has been so depleted by selling the best players, that the side can no longer compete effectively with other sides in the League? I had managed through sheer determination to keep the club alive in my two seasons as chief executive.

I did not sit in the stand at Kettering Town as an oracle waiting to be consulted. I took stock, outlined what could and should be done and in various ways I cleared club debts of £84,000. On the board there was too much timidity and complacency, not enough sense of adventure and imagination. There comes a time when beating one's head against a stone wall scrambles the brain – and for the sake of my peace of mind I had to leave, after almost two years' of daunting but invaluable experience. I still have great affection for Kettering and I hope that one day the people in the area will get the sort of club they deserve. They could have had it by now, if the board of directors had had vision.

I can take pride in what was achieved at Kettering during

my stay. I managed to leave the club in a much healthier position than I found it in and I reduced the loan on the Cash and Carry business by £10,000. To pay off the previous manager's contract, and keep the club going, John Nash and I each provided a loan, interest free, of £5,000. On the playing side, I had the satisfaction of bringing Billy Kellock out of the soccer wilderness when he was in dispute with Chelmsford and was no longer playing. Eventually, he was sold to Peterborough for £25,000. There was only one disagreement with my young assistant, Brian Thompson, who did not want to retain Gary Wood, a player in whom I recognised some special quality, which emerged when he was eventually sold for around £10,000 to Notts County.

There was much I would have liked to accomplish at Kettering and much that I could have achieved, for the club and the area, if I had been given the enthusiastic backing. As it all turned out, I went as far as I could go and knew that if I remained I would be on a treadmill, straining to keep in the same position. The way ahead is the only one that truly interests me. My only consolation was that at Kettering I left my successor with a far healthier situation than I inherited.

Five

Football started in the middle of the last century and if you read Dr Percy Young's account of the history of football you can see how so many people played important roles, not only in the establishing of clubs, but running them as a form of recreation and a diversion for the working class. In the early days most football clubs were run by committees. This system began to change at the turn of the century when a lot of clubs could have been liable or responsible for financial debts. Many turned themselves into limited companies. The condition of the professional footballer and his lot didn't really alter too much until 1885 when a 'bastardised profession' was made legal. Until then, footballers could only get money under the counter, they could not be paid for playing. It was decided to make it legal and for the first time in the game's history they started to play as professional footballers, in 1885. This was one of the contentious issues which began a split within the Establishment leading three years later to the formation of the Football League.

The professional footballer's lot didn't change at all during the rest of the last century. The football hierarchy fought vigorously through the early part of this century to prevent their organising themselves into a trade union. A serious attempt was made in 1898 to establish one but it took another nine years before it got off the ground. The lifestyle players are enjoying today is due to the pioneering work of the great Welsh international, Billy Meredith and a famous centre-half who played for Manchester United, Charlie Roberts, whose England career was cut short because of his union activities.

Unfortunately, because of the administrators' stranglehold, footballers found themselves depending on football's fixed wage for a living. There were a few serious attempts to improve conditions, but because we had two world wars, it wasn't until the late forties, and the early fifties, when Cliff Lloyd on 23

September 1953 became Secretary of the Professional Footballers' Union (as it was then known), that some progress was made in the treatment and the conditions of the professional footballer. When I came to England from Northern Ireland in August, 1957, the wage of the professional footballer was £17 in the playing season, and £15 in the close season. I was given my first contractual wage of £13 per week. At that stage it was quite a good wage, but after I had paid for my 'digs' and other expenses, like having to eat out every lunchtime, as my 'digs' only catered for breakfast and my evening meal, it didn't leave me with much. My only concern was that I wanted to play and get to the highest possible level, as a professional footballer. I even abandoned my apprenticeship as an electrician. I was lucky after a handful of games to get into the first team. It is remarkable, when I look back, how I was playing in the first team at Portsmouth FC for £13 per week, and yet a number of my colleagues were playing in the reserves and getting anything from £15 to £17 per week, because of the contracts they had signed for that particular season. It didn't cross the minds of my employers at that time to call me in during the season and give me an increase in salary. Perhaps the Football League wouldn't have allowed them to change my contract and give me an additional amount of money. I lost out financially but in April 1958, when I had kept my first team place from the previous October, I was called to the manager's office to be told that my salary was going to be increased by £2 per week, and that was for playing in the reserves! I said to him, 'But I don't play in the reserves.' I had been playing in the first team. He explained, 'Whilst you are playing in the reserves you should be getting the maximum amount of money.' He said that because I was a teenager, I wasn't or shouldn't expect really, the same as seasoned players. I said, 'Why not?' Not only am I your best player, but if I read the reports in the papers accurately, I seem to be provoking a lot of interest in the side.' I was eventually to be the only current International on the books. Teenagers normally don't make an impact on the professional game. They have to wait a number of years to be treated as the seasoned professionals. That's how it was in those days, less than 25 years ago.

Just after Mr Lever informed me of my increase in salary a

meeting of all the players and staff was called and Mr Lever announced sadly that he was no longer manager of Portsmouth FC. He thanked everyone for their support, and for the service they had rendered under him while he was manager. Not long afterwards I was selected to the Northern Ireland squad to go to Sweden to play in the World Cup, and made my debut against Czechoslovakia. It was an experience which added to my overall apprenticeship as a professional footballer. After that trip I thought I had come of age as a professional footballer. Looking back none of us even questioned the system. I was retained as a professional footballer and I was at the mercy of the football club like other players. If they wanted to retain me they did so. It was the first time I had experienced so much apprehension, so much concern and so much anxiety amongst married footballers, who had families and were living in club accommodation which tied them like serfs. The experience taught me that if I ever married the first thing I would do, if I had any money, would be to buy my own accommodation. A couple of players, Ray Crawford and Derek Weddle, were eventually given, or threatened with, eviction notices from their flats adjacent to the football club, because they had moved to other clubs, and had not found suitable accommodation. This caused a lot of bitterness in the dressing room. There was nothing the players could do about it. I realised there were not only seasoned professionals, there were experienced ex-international footballers, who were full of trepidation about whether they would be retained at the end of a season. It was at this stage that I first realised that footballers, who were professionals, were not treated with respect. I was treated better as a part-timer for four years, between 1953 and 1957, at Distillery in Ulster especially under the managership of Maurice Tadman. I compared the difference between being a part-timer in Northern Ireland and being a full-timer at Portsmouth FC, I didn't record my feelings and it is only now, writing this book, that I am putting on record my first experience of coming across bullies and tyrants operating a system prejudiced against the professional footballer.

It was going to be eight years before I came to the nerve centre of the administration, on behalf of the 2,500 footballers and so was able to do something to change the system. The public are not generally aware of the way footballers are and have been, treated. Even in the 1980s, they assume that these attitudes ceased to exist 20 or 30 years ago, but they still exist in the game. Footballers at many clubs, big and small ones, are still treated badly.

Freddie Cox, who succeeded Eddie Lever at Portsmouth, seemed to me to personify the unsympathetic 'boss', a manager whose attitudes and approach to the game set him apart from the players whose loyalty he needed but whose respect he did not care to encourage. One day he summoned me to his office. I knocked on the glass door and had to wait outside. He kept me waiting for some time before saying, 'Come in.' I entered and stood to attention. I was not asked to sit and although he had a pot of tea on his desk, he did not offer me a cup. In fact, in 25 years as a professional footballer, taking into account my years in Ireland, I have only enjoyed a cup of tea in a manager's office on two occasions. Only Joe Mercer at Villa and Gordon Clark at Peterborough extended this civility. I have known a number of team captains, the favourites of managers, to have enjoyed the facility many times.

Mr Cox questioned me about my 'audacity' in changing 'digs' without informing him. I put it to him that as I was paying for digs I felt I was entitled to decide where I should live. He couldn't understand this because he insisted that I should live in accommodation recommended by the club. I pointed out that I had lodgings for almost a season approved by the club and they did not create an environment where I wanted to stay. I wouldn't say I got my way, but I certainly didn't go to the digs chosen by the club. I eventually found my own. Mr Cox didn't take up my challenge that if they were prepared to pay for my digs, then I would live in those they recommended. If I had kow-towed and gone along with what the club decided for me, I would have been regarded as 'a good boy' in the eyes of the manager.

I played only two matches at the start of the 1958–59 season, before breaking an ankle. The management's view of my injury made me cynical and sceptical about some doctors' examinations and the medical advice given to players. When I broke my ankle it was diagnosed as only a bad sprain. It took three months before they found out that my ankle was broken. I broke it in August and I didn't play again in the first team until February, 1959. I had played only a few games after my injury when I was called to the manager's office to be greeted with a wan smile and be told by the manager that Blackburn Rovers wanted to sign me. He gave me some story about the club being short of money and I was the only one who could be sold. A quarter of a century later it's still the same old story! The professional footballer is but a prize animal to be bought and sold. They paid £4,000 for me and sold me for £12,000. I was pleased to go, knowing that if I stayed at Portsmouth my life would have been most uncomfortable. All I had experienced over my broken ankle left me with no desire to stay there and I was sceptical, to say the least, about some of the medical advice and attention given to players. God only knows how many players' careers have been shortened by faulty or careless medical diagnosis.

My move to Blackburn, though I did not relish the prospect of going to a northern industrial area, was fortuitous. The Blackburn players were much better than Portsmouth's. Surprisingly I did not have any advice from the players' union, although I paid my dues. There was no information and no assistance from the club delegates or from any of the senior professionals. I didn't know if I could have asked for any money to go to Blackburn Rovers. All I did know at the time was that if a player wanted a transfer he had to ask for one. By asking for a transfer a player's accrued share of benefits could be stopped because at that time for every year a player stayed at the club he got £150. If you were a 'good boy' after 5 years they made a song and dance by presenting you with a cheque for £750, (taxable). I received my accrued share which amounted to a few hundred pounds, but it wasn't the money which delighted me. I wanted to get out of an environment that didn't suit my personality. Freddie Cox and I were antipathetic and I could not make any progress under his management. I was looking forward to playing at Ewood Park. But after 3 or 4 games, I was aware I was not fitting into the Blackburn team. I seemed to have difficulty in sustaining games. I went down a couple of times very poorly and they found out my tonsils were septic. A specialist told me he did not know how I managed to do any training, let alone play football on Saturdays. My tonsils were removed in hospital. I had had this trouble for a couple of months before I left Portsmouth, where I would have a relapse after a Saturday game and I couldn't get out of bed until Tuesday or Wednesday, and by Thursday I was doing a little light training. I would play, and then, of course, the same thing happened to me for 7 or 8 weeks. I arrived at Blackburn Rovers, so run down and my system so weak, that it was soon diagnosed that immediate surgery was necessary. I didn't play again that season.

After coming out of hospital I welcomed the long break. In those days we had all of May, June, and most of July before reporting back for training. I recuperated for a couple of weeks in Ireland before spending the summer in Portsmouth. At this time I was rebelling against medical opinion and the Establishment. They had not diagnosed my broken ankle, not ascertained initially that I had septic tonsils and needed surgery. They thought I was skiving. When I reported back for preseason training I was a different person. My breathing was better and my ankle much stronger and I started playing well, scoring goals, and everyone was saying 'What a new bloke!' When some of the players were off form or the team itself was struggling, critics would say that they should have their tonsils removed and maybe they would play a lot better! This sort of talk was absurd, but I realised that football writers need some turns of phrase to be different from their colleagues. The team spirit and comradeship amongst the players at Blackburn Rovers was exceptionally good. The least popular player at Portsmouth, certainly in the dressing room, was the former English International Jimmy Dickinson, and it was remarkable that I soon realised the most unpopular player, certainly in the team at that time was the England captain and the skipper of Blackburn Rovers, Ronnie Clayton. I am not sure why he was unpopular. From the day I arrived I detected a certain amount of resentment. If you happen to be the England captain, you can detach yourself or become a degree aloof from the team. Whatever the factor was, unflattering remarks were at times made about Ronnie Clayton.

Going to the northern town with cobblestones, I was soon struck by the contrast. I had left behind the lovely, clean seaside resort of Southsea where I lived, and Portsmouth, and now I was training mornings and afternoons in a less salubrious atmosphere. Needing to wash my hair twice a day and not wanting all the bother in an incredibly warm summer – the best for 25 years – I went to the barber and said, 'I want it all off.' When he had taken most of it off, one side, he said, 'Are you sure?' and I said, 'Well, it's too late now,' and he took the clippers and clipped the rest of it off. My shaven head created a great deal of amusement, especially for Ally McLeod the former Scotland team manager, who took Scotland to the 1978 World Cup Finals.

I believe that this was the start of some people in the game thinking that anyone who did that, must be crackers – and on reflection, I suppose it did not always help when I expected to be taken seriously.

The light relief was needed to counteract some of the resentment and discontentment stemming from our antagonism towards inept management, directors and Ronnie Clayton, who didn't report sometimes until 10.30 am although the official time for reporting was 10.00 am. He had a newsagent's shop and was working in the shop which perhaps tells us something about the poor pay footballers were getting in those days. No doubt he may have needed extra security for himself and his family, so perhaps I was a little too hard on him. At the time I was probably swayed by the senior members' talk. They seemed to be jealous of the England team captain.

There wasn't too much discipline at the club and I felt that no-one took their football too seriously. There was a gentle approach to the game which was played with a lesser degree of competitiveness than it is today. This doesn't mean we didn't want to win. We certainly *did* want to win, but I was comparing the training I had had at Distillery for 4 years, and at Portsmouth. At Blackburn we had the nucleus of an outstanding side but I questioned our whole approach as far as application and professionalism were concerned. We rarely saw the manager, Dally Duncan. The only time we saw him was if we had reason to consult him in his office. Most weeks we saw him only on a Friday morning, or on a Saturday before the team went out, when sometimes he gave us a very short team-talk.

The role of a manager in the early days was feudalistic. He was detached from most of the players and was never in daily contact with the players at my first two clubs. When in the

Blackburn dressing room we spoke our minds about the lack of harmony and unity, the manager would get to know what was happening. I could not identify who told him what was going on, but someone did and that is why I have always been suspicious of trainers and team captains. Training was taken by Jack Weddle, the former Pompey player. Trainers always knew what the players were saying. Our remarks were often misconstrued. I was bothered because the right team spirit could have welded the side into one of the best in the league. Portsmouth players had fallen prey to old age. History proves that a team successful before it goes 'over the top' is never really dissected and taken apart to be re-conditioned, or new parts added. Such was the case of Portsmouth, still trying to live off the halcyon days from winning the championship twice in the late forties. This wasn't the case at Blackburn Rovers. Success had come in the early part of the century, and the last, but they were a renowned Cup-fighting team, and they had a lot of skilful footballers. They didn't, however, have the management and the administration to match the force of Manchester United, Wolverhampton Wanderers or Arsenal, or even Spurs for a few years. I questioned the old-fashioned training methods asking why we did this and why we should do that. This led to my being branded a troublemaker and a rebel. I was extremely frustrated. English players were not supposed to ask questions. They were not expected to have – or to voice – their own views about their clubs. As an Irishman, I could not accept these restraints. I had been encouraged by Maurice Tadman to speak my mind always while playing for Distillery in Belfast.

I had some setbacks in the season from pulled muscles. This came about because of conditions at Blackburn. I had not suffered from pulled muscles at Portsmouth or Distillery. The North having more rain from October or November onward, made the ground quite heavy. The trainer used to put studs about 2″ long in our boots. There was never much thought in preparing boots until later years. Having proved the theory of why I had a pulled muscle, I started to look after my own boots. Six months after I arrived at Blackburn I had a strange feeling that I would not stay long. It was not really 'my club'. Nor could Roy Vernon, the Welsh International, stand it and he was later transferred to Everton. I was destined to remain at

Blackburn for two years and four months. When a player moves from one club to another and then to a third club, people presume there is something wrong with him. As a part-timer in Northern Ireland, I only trained a couple of nights a week, in the playing season. The English League was a new world for me and I thought this is how it has gone on and this is the sort of attitude that has been indoctrinated into footballers, not only footballers, but trainers, management, administration, boards of directors, the FA the FL, and this attitude has been inherent now for a hundred years. Sad to say, the same attitudes prevail today. Most teams report at 10.00 am, they leave the ground at 12.30 pm and sometimes they come back in the afternoons. Some boards of directors meet once a month, some meet every couple of months some meet every three or four months, some meet twice a year. And there are the odd clubs that have only one meeting, their AGM. I am not sure what is right and what is wrong. What I *do* know is wrong, is the entire system of running professional football in this country. All my foregoing accounts and descriptions of my experiences at my early clubs are intended to illumine aspects of the game that can and do gravitate against its aims and ideals.

When I was transferred to Aston Villa, Blackburn Rovers had had me for two years and four months, and at the end they didn't want me any more and made 50 per cent profit on my transfer from one club to another. The trainer at the time, Ray Shaw, told me that it was amazing that although they had agreed a fee, in one room of a Manchester Hotel, the Blackburn manager was doing his damnedest to talk Joe Mercer out of having me. What they didn't realise at the time was that I had been to Joe Mercer's house and had agreed to join Aston Villa. As far as he was concerned and as far as I was concerned, it was only a formality. It was the first time I had come across a man I did not fully appreciate at the time. He was a track-suit manager, but he was a manager who over the next two years enlivened and then deflated me. The first year was marked by mishaps. I was involved in a very serious car crash, which set me back four months. The terrible winter of 1962–63 prevented our playing football for ten weeks and to make matters worse, I fell on the icy pavement outside my lodgings and twisted my knee, which meant my missing a lot of games. This prompted speculation that I was injury prone. Joe Mercer said to me, after I requested a meeting with him, that he did not listen to 80 per cent of the talk. I found that statement strange, why not 100 per cent? When you have been told something often enough, a little doubt can creep in, and rumours continued. I felt I was becoming a scapegoat for defeats. The irony is that I did not play in most of the games Villa lost and I did not play in the FA Cup match at Old Trafford which left the side demoralised. Nor did I play in the League Cup Final, when Villa were beaten in the two legs by rivals Birmingham City.

After two years at Villa Park, I was unwanted and for the first time in my career I was officially put on the transfer list. A few clubs made enquiries. Eventually, disillusioned, I went to Peterborough United in the Third Division, which proved to be a salutary experience. Before leaving Villa Park, I had sought meetings with the chairman (Chris Buckley) and had tried to put to him my point of view, which he accepted. It was a paradoxical situation. He wanted me to stay, the supporters wanted me to stay and so did the shareholders and season ticket holders. Only the manager wanted me to go. Later on, I realised that he was really doing me a favour, because when I was discarded by Villa I began to take myself more seriously and to reflect on my future in the game. I have given fuller accounts of my Aston Villa days and of my experiences at other clubs in previous books, Attack! and The Sash He Never Wore.

The year I joined Aston Villa, 1961, was an auspicous one for professional footballers. It brought the abolition of the maximum wage. Harry Leyland, a PFA delegate at Blackburn and a member of the PFA management committee, had encouraged the players to make the trips to Manchester and listen to the points of view about why we should be prepared to strike to get improved wages. In getting the maximum wage abolished, we learned that only by sticking together and having a concerted campaign, could anything worthwhile be achieved.

Not long after I had been invited to join the PFA management committee, Cliff Lloyd told me that the committee would have settled for £30 a week, representing a 50 per cent rise. The amount offered was £25 a week and the FL management committee would not budge. The PFA management committee were prepared to accept £30 a week, a rise of £10. I sometimes reflect what would have happened if they had accepted £30 a week. That is one of the game's imponderables. Perhaps further enlightenment on the subject will come when Cliff Lloyd writes his memoirs. Around this time I began to take a greater interest in PFA affairs. Generally, its communications with clubs were poor and in some cases, non-existent. At Villa Park, I did not even know who was the union delegate.

Until I became actively involved with the PFA I did not know that since his appointment, Cliff Lloyd had been working patiently since 1953, and with a great deal of exasperation, to build up for the big explosion known as the Eastham case, which hinged on 'restraint of trade'. George Eastham, of Newcastle United, had wanted to join Arsenal. His club had refused. Though he was granted a transfer he felt he had to see the matter through in a court of law. The PFA had set aside enough money to fight a test case on behalf of players tied to clubs when their contracts had ended. Mr Justice Wilberforce, on 4 July 1963, ruled in effect that contracts signed by members of the PFA were illegal and that the retention provisions were in restraint of trade.

I always felt it unfair that a footballer could be held against his will, amounting to moral, financial and legal rape. The game is about players – yet footballers are 'raped'. They are continually 'raped' by their contractual obligations. Rape by definition is doing something to the opposite (or the same) sex without consent. A majority of footballers today are held at clubs against their consent. *Ergo*, rape!

Until the Eastham case, we felt at the PFA that nothing could be done about it. Bearing in mind that the PFA (originally the Players' Union) was constituted in 1907, 56 years was a long time to wait for this improvement. If it had not been for Cliff Lloyd we might have had to wait much longer, perhaps another 56 years. But clubs could still hold players at the end of their contracts, even if they could not offer the minimum of £8 a week. It took another 12 years and a lot of heartache and soul-searching before a newly established PFA negotiating committee got down to an item on the agenda entitled Complete Freedom of Contract. Between 1963 and 1975 we saw changes in the relationship between club and player. Perhaps I should say manager and player. The player, when he becomes a manager, often forgets the attitudes which prevailed against him as a player. All at once, he prefers to go along with the system. Many managers who, as players, would have welcomed what the PFA was trying to achieve, set themselves against the negotiations, alleging that the PFA's proposals would 'ruin the game as we know it'. In the course of many negotiations, we established that a player should have ten per cent of his transfer fee. Afterwards, we agreed that five per cent should go to the player and the other five per cent to augment the players' provident fund. Little did we realise that transfer fees were going to rocket and that five per cent of all transfer fees would be more than enough to underwrite the provident fund. It is pleasing that star players, while getting a bit of money for themselves in transfer deals, also helped their fellow professionals who never figured in the transfer market, by agreeing to contribute five per cent of their share to the fund.

I must admit I was taken aback to find that the money given to the FL regarding transfer fees was in excess of the premium paid to underwrite the provident fund. All of the money which accrued was eventually divided among the 92 clubs. I was annoyed, not because the money was given back to the clubs, but because it took us so long to find out about it. The FL's management committee have not always been as forthcoming as they might have been.

Six

Now it is time to consider how football clubs should be run, under a different form of administration. Under the present system which has prevailed for the past 50 years, the directors appoint a chairman, the chairman appoints a manager and the manager appoints his staff, regardless of how good or bad the manager has been as a player and regardless of his managerial abilities from a business point of view. The manager is immediately put into the hot seat, under pressure to produce results within a particular period, which can range from weeks to a couple of seasons and if he does not provide the goods, out he goes, while those who have appointed him remain where they are.

When I tried to acquire Walsall FC I had in mind a different set-up, in which at first I would have had overall control. In the early stages I would have run the entire administration, not out of a vain desire to be the Orson Welles of football, but to establish priorities and lay the foundations of a more democratic system. In time, I would have hand-picked the right people so that various responsibilities and duties could be delegated to them. I firmly contend that successful management depends on wise delegation. I would have worked in conjunction with the local Press, knowing that its close interest in a football club is essential. At Kettering, during the club's successful FA Cup run, the local newspaper was strike-bound for a long time and the lack of exposure in the Press had a depressing effect on attendances. I would have appointed someone to seek sponsorship and look after advertising and publicity. I was so convinced these ideas could come to fruition at Walsall that at the PFA annual general meeting in November 1974, I approached Terry Venables, who was with me on the PFA management committee, and told him I might want him to look after the team affairs of a football club if I could get it. I asked if he would be interested and he said he would be willing to discuss it with me. He would have been the right person, but that is another story. What might have been?

I have thought for some time that the structure of a football club under the old system should be two-tier, with a general manager looking after club affairs in conjunction with a manager. A team manager's sole reponsibility would be the selection of the team and the procurement of players, as well as a scouting system. All team matters and team affairs would be his responsibility. If I have selected the right man, I would say to him, 'Regardless how the results go initially, you are here for three years because I believe you are the best man to look after the team affairs.' This would give him a sense of security and relieve him of the anxiety under which managers have to operate. It would also help him to establish a better relationship with his players.

When a player is having problems with his manager over a financial settlement of his contract an impasse occurs and the manager tells the player, 'I'll put it to the board.' What he says to the board on the player's behalf is open to conjecture, because the player is never present to hear what is being said. He sees him the following week and is informed there hasn't been a board meeting because the chairman wasn't available or certain members of the board were not available. Then there is stalemate and the player feels distracted to a point of frustration. He bites his tongue and the next week sees the manager again, the manager says, 'Come and see me next Friday.' He goes again and finds that the manager is on holiday and will not be back for two or three weeks. This causes more frustration which builds up to bitterness and resentment. The manager should tell the player that he will be away and will see him when he returns. When the manager comes back from holiday the player has probably not had his own holiday because of wanting to stay around to sort out his contract. The manager says he has not had time to see the chairman, or the chairman is away on holiday. So it goes on, from weeks to months.

Chairmen often leave important matters to managers. In turn, managers delegate responsibilities to secretaries and the upshot over the years is that club secretaries, usually anonymous men whose offices are hard to penetrate, have gathered about themselves increasing influence and power, far more than is appropriate for the position. Players are often caught between chairman, manager and secretary, unsure whom to consult.

At Leicester City and later with Wolves, I saw this happen frequently. Players are put in a bad state of mind and this can affect their concentration in training. At one time I had no fewer than six footballers in this troubled state at Wolves. I did my best to persuade them that everything could and would be sorted out smoothly, to their satisfaction. It should have been possible to resolve such problems on the spot, in the manager's office, but if McGarry had the ability to communicate with his players to inspire confidence, he did not show it. A player in dispute with his club could not be sure he was being given all the facts.

The management committee of the PFA tried, on a national scale, to get to grips with the problem and 18 months were spent on negotiations with the Football League management committee before a package deal was drawn up. But the FL committee did not have a mandate to introduce it and after it had been thrown out by the clubs at their annual meeting an independent tribunal was eventually set up to settle disputes between players and their clubs. Players then knew they would get a fair hearing and a just deal. The tribunal became necessary because clubs could not see it was in their own interest to look after their players, making sure they were happy and contented off the pitch, with the terms of their contracts.

It should be up to a general manager who has direct contact with the board, to negotiate, so players would not feel bitter against their team manager. If it were not his responsibility, a player would be in a better frame of mind and would respect the team manager more, knowing that his contract was not his responsibility. If there is an impasse or a state where negotiations have not been fully agreed, the general manager should bring a player before the Board of Directors to have the opportunity to speak to the people who control and run the club. They might have legitimate or convincing reasons beyond his knowledge for his not getting what he wants or is requesting. If players know they have been treated fairly, truthfully and with sincerity and consideration) they would be more inclined to compromise and a settlement could be reached.

At Wolverhampton Wanderers I often mediated between the manager and players. I talked to the manager because he wouldn't listen to the players, especially about their grievances. I was only talking about a few pounds a week and not the large sums that are discussed today!

A general manager, hopefully an ex-player with some business experience, would need flair and ability to discuss with the team manager what they could budget, what the players salaries should be and the bonus structure. This would reduce the chances of a player falling out with his team manager and not giving his best in training and on match days. A typical recent example of this occurred at Nottingham Forest when Garry Birtles was told by the management that his concentration was elsewhere. His performances reflected distractions off the pitch, but the situation was not created entirely by the player.

Most managers would frown on a two-tier system, without even considering its advantages. They are locked within an old system and assume, because it has existed for a long time, that things cannot be done in a different and much better way. At heart, they look with disdain on anything they believe threatens their overall position. It is extraordinary that so few managers see that a two-tier system, with a general manager and a team manager, would relieve the team managers of financial anxieties and problems for which they have not been trained to tackle. They would be able to get on with what they know, or should know, best – the game itself. Since I came to England in 1957 I have encountered only a few, rare managers with the ability to handle players. Players, that is, as people. To handle players sensitively, instead of as numbers on a pitch, requires special abilities of leadership.

There is a lingering attitude among League managers that players should be 'kept down' and not given much latitude. Their thinking is that if players are given the freedom and individuality which applies in other professions, they will get beyond themselves, make excessive demands and resist discipline. There is no evidence for this prejudice, only the prejudice itself. Players have always had to battle for better conditions and opportunities. Through the PFA, they have had to assert the justice of their causes, making a little progress here, a little there, pushing on gradually to get their just entitlements. When

I was representing players in disputes with their clubs I learned the Machiavellian art of duplicity, gamesmanship and a degree of cunning, to make sure that the players putting their trust in me, emerged with fair deals.

To mention a few examples out of the many in my years representing players, at independent tribunals, I will start with the Ian Bowyer case at Nottingham Forest. It had elements of farce and some guile and bluff were needed to resolve the dispute, which the player by his own efforts, had been unable to do before the matter was referred to the independent tribunal.

Nottingham Forest offered him a new contract of less favourable terms, which meant in effect that he qualified for a free transfer. When this was confirmed by the Football League and the club realised its error, which could only have been a mix-up between the manager and secretary, a new contract was offered to him.

The player pointed out that this would leave him on the original terms, making no allowance for the rising cost of living and new commitments at home, after his wife had given birth to twins. He had been with Forest for almost two seasons, after his transfer from Orient in October 1973. The option on his contract expired on 30 June 1975. Commenting on the revised offer of first team appearance money and bonuses, Ian asked what would happen if he were injured and out of the first team. Furthermore, there were three months of the year when no matches were played.

Because he was given a free transfer Forest appealed to the independent tribunal and a hearing was arranged at the Great Western Hotel in London, under the chairmanship of Sir John Wood. Sir Matt Busby represented the Football League and Cliff Lloyd the PFA. Brian Clough turned up at the hotel wearing his tracksuit and running shoes, looking as if he had just sprinted across from the training ground. Whether he was deliberately trying to convey an air of nonchalance I don't know, but I recollected his sartorial appearance on a later occasion when he disciplined Larry Lloyd for not wearing the club's blazer on tour in a European Cup match, thus confirming my belief that there is a set of rules for managers and another for players, summed up in a managerial phrase, 'Don't do as I do, do as I say.'

While the tribunal members were getting ready in a room of the hotel, the three of us – Brian Clough, Ian Bowyer and myself – met in an adjoining room. Immediately I discovered that Mr Clough was apprehensive. He said to me, 'I don't want to go before the tribunal.' I told him, 'You don't have to.' He looked startled and asked what I meant. When I suggested to him that we could settle the matter there and then and avoid going in front of the tribunal, he readily agreed. As there were others waiting to appear before the tribunal, we could not talk in confidence in the room. But there was no ante-room, only a corridor. While Mr Clough waited in the room, I took Ian into the corridor and asked him, 'What do you want?' We discussed the situation and I advised him to leave everything to me. We then went back into the room and Mr Clough came with me into the corridor, where I told him what he must have known, that he had an unhappy player on his hands. After I had stressed how insecure Ian felt, Mr Clough improved on the offer. It was not good enough. I said, without any enthusiasm, I would put it to him. We returned to the room and I came out again, into the corridor, with Ian. For a couple of minutes, as if we were discussing the offer, we chatted about the weather, Ian's family and anything else that occurred to us. Anything except the offer.

The shuttle service continued, with us going back to the room and Mr Clough and I coming out to resume negotiations in the corridor. 'I don't know what you've done to him,' I said, confidentially. 'He's very unhappy ...' By this time the tribunal were ready to start the proceedings. I thought we were making progress and a satisfactory agreement could be reached without the tribunal. I felt we had the advantage, because Mr Clough was anxious to avoid appearing before the tribunal and now, if he wished to avoid it, he would have to come up quickly with a much better offer.

I told the tribunal that there was a reasonable chance of settling the dispute and would they mind giving us a little more time to negotiate? They were happy to grant the request while they took tea.

Again, in the corridor, while Ian waited in the room, Mr Clough improved on the offer, making now nearly double Ian's old wage. Manager and player again exchanged places, one waiting in the room, while the other spoke with me in the corridor. I knew we nearly had him and that the player would get what I considered to be a fair salary. But there was a psychological advantage in not appearing to rush, even though the comings and goings, between the room and the corridor, were starting to take on the appearance of a Feydeau farce. Ian and I killed a few minutes with idle smalltalk and I even resorted to making comments about the state of the wallpaper, which needed replacing. Then I went back with him into the room and brought Mr Clough into the corridor. 'Brian,' I said, 'he's adamant. I've stressed to him the importance of your gesture and he is willing to come down a few pounds. I'll tell you what I'll do – I'll urge him to settle for an amount below what he has been determined to get.'

The stakes were on the table, but really it was a game of bluff and gamesmanship. Mr Clough upped the offer and Ian could hardly believe it. He would have settled for far less, but as his representative I had to look after his true interests and not allow his nervousness to dictate unfavourable terms below what I knew could be achieved. If it meant outwitting Mr Clough, well, that was not the player's doing, it was mine. I was concerned with the player's welfare and security and knowing how personal grievances can disturb a player's performances on the pitch, I was really doing Brian Clough a favour in getting him to put forward an offer which would ease Ian Bowyer's mind after the low expectations with which he had come to the hearing.

The tribunal were delighted by the outcome. Mr Clough shook hands with the members and was obviously relieved he had not been obliged to state the club's case in front of them. But when the three of us were in the corridor he emphasised with a clenched fist that none of the other Forest players should know that Ian was now on the same wage as Terry Curran. The fact that Ian stayed with Forest for seven years vindicates the stand I took. He was worth a lot to Forest, who sold him to Sunderland for seven times his original value.

Another example of players in disputes that could easily have been resolved, with more managerial understanding and compassion, was at Hull, where eight first team players had grievances and were seeking the tribunal's impartial judgment. One player, Roy Greenwood, had a transfer market price of £150,000, but his wage was only £28 a week, out of proportion to his valuation, which should have set his wage at about £200 a week. He would have been happy with £60 a week.

I was looking forward to representing the players at the tribunal, not least because of the antipathy between the manager, Terry Neill, and myself. When he left to become manager of Tottenham, all but one player, Roy Greenwood, settled their differences within a short while of the arrival of the new manager, John Kaye. Terry Neill should have treated his players at Hull better. They were not in dispute for the sake of causing trouble, but through justified grievances which a manager ought to resolve in everyone's interest, including his own.

At West Ham, under Ron Greenwood's management, Bobby Ferguson (goalkeeper) and Trevor Brooking were in dispute. Both were reasonably happy with their contracts, but unhappy about the option period. Mr Greenwood wanted them to take his word that their contracts would be renegotiated at the end of the first period. The players wanted a written undertaking, asking what might happen if the manager – one of the most sincere and trustworthy in the game – dropped dead, were sacked or stepped in front of a bus. During talks on the issue he took me outside and said he would agree to remove the word 'option'. My respect and admiration for him increased, but he could have done this many months before.

Fewer players would be in dispute and relationships between them and their clubs would be eased if the football authorities had accepted the PFA's proposal for players at the end of their contracts to become free agents. This would end the farce of cheques changing hands, not for players but for the right to register them. A king's size ransom is often demanded for players who are paid a pittance.

The PFA, under my chairmanship, suggested a multiplying factor when determining transfer fees. By basing the fee on a player's salary, his age and the status of the club he would be joining, transfer deals could be kept to reasonable proportions. Managers could not understand what we were trying to do. They had become so conditioned by the old system, they could only react as if we were trying to undermine the game itself.

So they formed a resistance group and beat off our proposals.

They have behaved like daring young men in worn-out flying machines, soaring into the realms of financial fantasy, breaking the £1 million sound-sense barrier and now they are crash diving. Club after club in the 1980–81 season has reported crises and the most common phrase of the season has not been 'over the moon' but 'the fight for survival'. The moonshine has ended and the cosmic rays, from the outer space between managers' and directors' ears, are burning away the foundations of clubs throughout the League.

They are blaming falls in attendance, but have not blamed themselves. They have not adequately explained why attendances have fallen. The 'guilty' men have not stood up to count the empty seats and spaces on the terraces. They continue to sit in their insulated boxes and blow cigar smoke in the boardrooms. In the heat of the battle for survival, they are miles and years behind the front line. Having squandered fortunes, they were wondering where the money has gone and why too little is coming into the game. They remind me of those East Anglian landowners who cut down the trees and hedgerows to provide more open land and then found the wind blew away the top soil, leaving vast acres of ground barren.

All players, and especially those with a high transfer market value, need treating with respect. The attitude of present day management is a relic of how players were treated 20, 30, and in some cases 40 years ago. Many managers are old-fashioned and committed to ancient ideas. They will not change unless a new system is forced on them. They haven't the vision or the ability to initiate changes for themselves, which is why I am an arch critic of the present system. When young ex-players become managers they soon acquire old ideas, the present system does not train footballers to become managers able to communicate with spectators, how to take the Press into their confidence and be honest with sports reporters. Nor are they trained how to liaise with directors of football clubs, to get together with them and discuss policies to explain what they are going to do over a two or three year programme and to implement them. The present system, or structure of football today, doesn't act in the interest of the game. Spectators and players get a raw deal. If extra money were found, especially from the government, and it were spread among clubs subject to pre-determined, and stringent conditions, clubs would have to show greater responsibility in their spending. They would be discouraged from squandering money on 'white elephant' stands and on unrealistically high transfer deals. Time and again we see clubs getting themselves deeper and deeper into debt by trying in vain to buy instant success. I cannot think of a team this century which has been able to buy success. Sometimes a club achieves success, if only temporary, by two or three astute signings and blending newly acquired players with the established nucleus, but for every success there are a score of failures.

Success in the long run means careful planning and the adoption of shrewdly thought-out policies. This requires good business judgment, sound administration and all the back-up facilities necessary for running a confident and consistent side. This is why I propose a two-tier management system. The sort of two-tier system established at a number of clubs is an administrative fraud, nothing more than a sop to supporters and a means of disguising the shame of a good and loyal servant being kicked out of his managerial job. The title of 'general manager' is often given to someone whom it would be imprudent, from a public relations point of view, to dismiss. To give one example, rather than sack Ron Greenwood, West Ham kicked him upstairs. The gods later smiled on him. His great piece of luck was his ability to handle the national side when the FA invited him to take over on a temporary basis. He had a reasonable amount of success to justify his keeping the position, but this sort of situation is exceptional. The FA and the Football League have been negligent in not implementing proper courses, of varying degrees, for senior players in the late twenties and early thirties. Potential managers, while they are still players, should be given the opportunity to learn how to manage a team and to cope with other facets that go with the running of a club.

Seven

At the start of this book I asked: What is a football club? A football club today is big business, it is big opportunity. It has popular and commercial potential but the people who control it have not changed throughout this century. We shall continue to stumble from one crisis to another, we shall continue to have a situation where a number of issues will become controversial whether it is the pools not paying enough money or TV is not paying enough money, or 'why' the government should be putting money into football. All the reports published over the last 15 years contain all the necessary answers. All the FA and FL need do is implement them. Then we would see tremendous changes in the game. The FA and the FL would have to come under one umbrella, along with the PFA to bring a degree of professionalism into the administration over many issues. There are not many ex-players, household names or not, playing major roles in the administration or in the running of the game, which I find strange and ironical. It is the only industry in which one can accumulate 30 or 40 years experience, and then at the end of the day, it is allowed to go to waste. If it were not for the Professional Footballers' Association starting a minicourse at the end of a season for about sixteen players, giving them some sort of preparation in management, and other aspects of the game, the situation would be far bleaker. Why have we never gone outside the game to recruit people, whether on a consultancy or a professional basis, to pass on their experience and wisdom in the interest of the game? Experts are needed to improve the standards and the quality of administration and of management. If we did this there is no doubt that one day, we would go back to the government and say, 'Now we have put our house in order and we feel that football is producing so much money for you, we are entitled to some of it back.' While the FA and the Football League clubs fail to overhaul themselves, there will never be any extra money coming from government sources.

Under the present system there is need for a general manager at each club, and perhaps one day becoming managing director, paid an adequate salary for the responsibilities he undertakes. Most directors in the game are not too successful as football directors, so it would be unlikely to find a potential managing director among them. One has only to attend the AGM of the FA and the FL to see the chaos and hear the nonsense talked about the important issues facing football. The biggest issue of all is survival. Radical changes will not occur without a change of attitude at clubs where court favourites hang around enjoying the social environment, which is their only interest. In the First Division an average of 20,000 or 25,000 people support a club and for their loyalty and enthusiasm get only a raw deal. Football clubs do not realise what goodwill and support they have from the public. Enthusiastic supporters help run lotteries, some sponsors buy the strips and provide the footballs, firms take out long leases on boxes or short leases on the executive boxes and yet the return for their investment is not much. The response they get from managements and directors is often discouraging, failing to match their own voluntary efforts. At boardroom levels and in managers' offices, attitudes are more minimising than expansionist. Instead of enlarging their concepts of how to run football, they devise ways of narrowing them.

Some managers and administrators have called for fewer clubs, not excluding their own from the League, of course! I would like to see a League of one hundred clubs, adding to the present ninety-two, four from the north and four from the south of the Premier leagues. The set-up as I envisage it, would then be a league of five tables, with 20 clubs in each: first, second and third divisions and a fourth division north and fourth division south. To increase competition and interest, I would suggest a promotion and relegation system of four up and down in the first, second and third divisions, two from each of the fourth divisions. These and the following proposals, I will continue to enlarge upon as the text goes on.

Were I football's overlord, I would restore Northern Premier and Southern Premier Leagues, so that the winner of each automatically changed places with the bottom club in the respective fourth divisions. This would end the situation which crops up every season when non-League clubs ambitious to join the League have to go out of their way to persuade League chairmen to smile benevolently on them and rarely succeed in their blandishments. The revised system, apart from being more democratic and fair, would encourage a team ejected from the League to pick itself up by the bootlaces and strive for re-entry.

I wish club directors could see the practical logic of this scheme, instead of re-enacting the same scenario, season after season, confounding the hopes and aspirations of worthy non-League clubs and giving their blessings to unworthy League sides whose performances should disqualify them from League membership. But then, what can one expect of directors who pay too little attention to the realities of the game and prefer to bask in the social limelight?

Knowing too little about the game, they leave it in the hands of managers and secretaries who are not equipped for day-to-day administration. Maladministration and inefficiency in the football industry are rife. When a cash crisis occurs or when there is an administrative problem through over-staffing, the automatic response is to reduce the playing staff. This is a cardinal mistake. Should a club reduce its playing staff to a basic level, one or two injuries could deplete it. And a reduction in playing staff would mean corresponding reductions in the coaching and office staff. Economies should not always begin and end with players, the most valuable assets.

The stronger the playing staff, the more efficient it is. Most directors do not know much about the transfer of a player, either to their club or from their club. The first they know about it, in many cases is when they read about it in the newspapers, or hear about it on TV or radio. I know a chairman of a football club whose manager was involved in a transfer of £250,000 and the first he knew of it was when he came home and his wife said to him, 'Oh did you know that we bought Joe Bloggs from such and such a club?' This situation is senseless and is not in the interest of any club whether the First Division or the Fourth Division. Five years ago before the really big fees, a manager of a club in the Midlands wanted a certain player, who he thought could do a great job for his team in the First Division. His offer of £60,000 was laughingly rejected. A week later he upped the offer to £80,000. Again it was scorned. He upped it again to £100,000. Within another week he upped it yet again to £120,000. He then made another bid. At this stage another club came in from the north and the bidding went on backwards and forwards. The original manager dropped out at £200,000 and the player was sold for £220,000. I am convinced that if he had offered a reasonable fee of £100,000–£120,000 in the first place he would have got the player. This is why I believe a two-tier management is essential. A general manager as a link between the Board and the team manager would be able to sit down and look at a matter rationally and constructively before offering the sort of fee a club can afford to pay.

In the past five years transfer fees have not only gone through the roof, they have soared even beyond the stratosphere into some never-never land, which is at least apposite, because many players are bought on the never-never system and are still being paid for when they have been sold again to another club. In the world outside football this is a breach of the law and a criminal offence.

It is extraordinary that they seem unable to learn from the follies and failures of one another. There are plenty of object lessons. Sunderland, Manchester United and Manchester City for instance, have at critical times in their history tried to buy success.

A successful side can go through traumas trying to maintain its reputation when the players who have brought success are 'going over the hill'. It can easily panic and rush into the transfer market to fill the gaps. Wolverhampton Wanderers, Tottenham, Arsenal, Leeds, Nottingham Forest ... these are some of the clubs in the post-war years who have failed to find the right replacements at the right time to maintain their successful runs. Liverpool are an outstanding example of shrewd planning, both Bill Shankly and his successor, Bob Paisley, knowing how and when to strengthen the side, with the right mixture. Liverpool have bought wisely from the lower divisions and introduced individualists among the home-bred players in the squad.

When, at the start of this book, I suggested that directors should be required to invest certain sums, interest-free, as a condition of directorship, I explained that this would encourage them to take their positions more seriously. I repeat this assertion in connection with clubs which desperately try to buy success and fail miserably. Directors who had put substantial amounts of their own money into their clubs would be more likely to restrain free-spending managers and themselves. They would be forced to appraise their club's financial position and take care not to squander resources. We would soon be able to distinguish between good and bad directors.

Bad directors who are only there for what they can gain socially and for perks and those who are not playing any significant role, would fall by the wayside, then we would get directors with a commitment, and not only a financial commitment, but a passion to try to make the industry a thriving one, rather than a contracting industry. Players and managers mostly feel that the directors in the main are a joke. When Len Shackleton wrote a book on football, he entitled a page: 'What directors know about football' and left the page blank. It was a joke but realistically based. If directors really did know much about the game, football wouldn't be in the perilous state it is today. In their ignorance they have perpetuated a system which holds up progress, diminishes public interest, and stops the turnstiles clicking short of break-even point. Football could exist and get along far better and more efficiently if the responsibility were taken from the administrators. A lot of directors, chairmen and managers will frown upon these ideas because in their conceit they believe they know everything there is to know about football. At the time of the World Cup in West Germany in 1974 I asked a few managers at a football writers' dinner in London if they would be going to observe the different training programmes and the different styles of play among the international teams. One manager said to me, 'Well, what have we got to learn there? There's nothing we can learn from them.' This is the sort of attitude which undermines the game. A lot of people in football today are not capable of examining themselves closely and constructively. They cannot say to themselves, 'Maybe we are not doing things right – maybe it is time to reappraise our methods.' They are unable or unwilling to reassess the administration to see what could be done to make things better for the players and the spectators and everyone else associated with the game. I was disappointed with the Work

Study Committee set up a few years ago to meet three or four times a year to discuss issues informally and constructively not to implement anything, but to 'throw it around' for discussion! There has not been a meeting since 1971. This sort of lethargy prevails in football today.

Football's misfortune is that there are too few people involved in it for what they can put into it. When constructive proposals are made by the PFA they invariably accuse the players' organisation of being disruptive. For instance, when under my chairmanship, the PFA expressed its concern over what threatened to be an unrestricted flow of foreign players into the English League, Cliff Lloyd and I were pilloried for taking the stand we did. It was difficult, in the heated arguments relayed in the Press, to make ourselves understood. All we asked, was to protect English football by making sure that foreign players were properly vetted before being allowed to join League clubs. Our fear was that a lot of money could be sent out of the country and lost to the League, on unknown quantities. We were not against foreign players, only opposed to all and sundry coming here and competing against home-produced players, regardless of their reputations and talent. We proposed that only those who had played for their countries and were of proven ability should be given permits. Managers and scouts, unable to travel to distant countries to study players wanting to come here, could be easily misled. They could assume that because a player came from Brazil or Argentina, he must be good, according to the World Cup image of Brazilian and Argentinian players. Our plea was for discretion and caution, to avoid an influx which could imperil the grass roots of English League football. There was nothing racial or xenophobic in the PFA's attitude, but our views were misrepresented by those who wanted to throw open the doors, as if to continentalise or internationalise our game. Many foreign players want to play in the English League not for the money – they can earn more in their own countries – but because the standard of competition is so good and healthy. They are attracted by the high quality of the English League, and the commitment it carries for 46 weeks of the year and its world-wide reputation at domestic level.

The PFA took its views to the Department of Employment in order to protect clubs and young, unestablished players who coming through from junior teams and schools, could have found diminishing opportunities if there were a surfeit of foreign players arriving every season. The likes of Ardiles have brought fresh vigour and interest to the game and no one would question his value to Spurs and the incentive he gives to youngsters to raise their standards. His arrival in the English League illustrated the PFA's case, the logic of which has since been proved and generally accepted.

Administrators and legislators cannot bring themselves to accept that the PFA means well and is only concerned with the state of the industry. Contrary to the feelings, thinking and philosophy of the club chairmen, managers, and directors, players are not only interested in getting bigger salaries, bigger bonuses, and being totally selfish. This is not always the case. They are primarily concerned with security, first team football, and playing to the best of their ability. I have been obsessed with changing the structure of professional football so that at the end of a footballer's career he will be able to decide whether he wants to stay in the game at administrative level. No obstacle should be put in his way; under the present situation a professional footballer is inhibited from exploiting his true potential, his managerial potential or his administrative potential. The FA and the FL do not make much of a contribution to preparing footballers to become managers. Unless they do so, we will have situations where managers will get the sack because they are not managerial material. If they had courses on management in the fullest sense of the word players themselves would realise either halfway through or three quarters of the way through, that they are not managerial material.

Before setting out on his managerial career, Don Revie took a 'crash course' and asked a few managers for advice. He sought the counsel of Sir Matt Busby who told him, 'Treat them [the players] honestly and never lie to them. That way they'll do anything for you and when that happens you can do anything you want.' I'm not sure if he did or not. More than a decade ago I wrote that there were managers who in the army would be blustering NCO's, managers who were so remote from their players that they resembled Trappist monks, managers who had so little authority that the players managed them! This is applicable today. Of course, there are managers with imagination and foresight, diplomacy and sincerity, but finding them is like coming across a first and rare edition or an unusual stamp. If a manager cannot inspire his players when they are feeling low after defeat, he ought to find another vocation. I remember Bill Shankly's reaction some years ago when Liverpool were trounced in Holland in a European Cup match. He said to the Press, 'My lads would beat them ten—nil at Anfield.' This renewed their confidence. They knew he had not lost faith in them and that he was not bluffing to conceal his disappointment. He meant what he said and the players knew he would not say anything he did not mean.

This is the secret of successful management, the ability to make players feel 10 feet tall, even in defeat; to inspire and stimulate them. It does not mean passing over defects, ignoring weaknesses and living in cloud-cuckoo land; it means carefully building up a team and making everyone believe he is an essential part of the team and it means instilling club pride, particularly among the reserves and third team players.

A manager who passes his players in the corridor or in the street without a word, is a pompous fool; a manager who imposes tiresome restrictions without explanation is an arrogant fool; a manager who mistakes cussedness for discipline and aloofness for dignity fools himself. He will never get players to play their hearts out and he will find they are more interested in getting away than in winning honours for the club.

Having given my reasons for not wanting to manage a League club under the prevailing system, it seems hypocritical and contradictory that I should have applied to be manager of my old club, Wolves, after the dismissal of Sammy Chung. There were special and extenuating circumstances. One weekend in November 1978, I addressed a Sunday meeting of referees at Goodison Park and stayed overnight before going to Manchester for my last AGM of the PFA as chairman. During the meeting I was inundated with phone calls from the Press and various people asking for my reaction to crowd demonstrations at Molineux the previous Saturday. I was told that they had kept up a vociferous chant, 'The Doog for manager!' I had to ask that no more calls be put through to me. When I returned home in the evening, I was inundated with calls and messages. Obviously, there was a strong groundswell of opinion among

Wolves supporters, calling on me to apply for the job. Even so, I was still reluctant to make an application. Then my wife, whose judgment I have always respected, said it was my duty to apply; my duty to supporters. I had to keep faith with them. Before finally making up my mind, I got in touch with John Richards and asked him whether he thought the players, most of whom had been my team-mates, would accept me as manager. He assured me there would be no problem, that they would be happy about it. So I decided to make a formal application.

After the Molineux demonstrations, the local newspaper asked the club chairman, Harry Marshall, if I was being considered for the post. He deflected the enquiry by saying that I had not applied. He could not bring himself to say 'No' because in spite of what they profess, chairmen, directors and managers really do care what supporters think of them. They want to be popular. After the sacking of Bill McGarry, Sammy Chung had been Harry Marshall's choice. But I knew that he had been manager in name only, and that the management of the club had been conducted by the chairman. If Don Howe had accepted an invitation to manage Wolves, Sammy would have been his NO. 2. In my opinion he demeaned himself by accepting this proposition which failed to come about when Don Howe decided that Molineux was not for him. The team had failed to live up to promises and expectations, so Chung, like many other managers, had to be the sacrificial goat. Now, to all intents and purposes, the position was vacant again. Or was it?

Remembering that the club had previously denied knowledge of my application for shares, even though it had been sent by recorded delivery (the application mysteriously turned up when I threatened to go to the Post Office to demand an investigation), I decided to deliver my application for the manager's job through my solicitor. He took it to the ground personally. The response was a phone call on the Friday morning from the club secretary, Phil Shaw, who said, 'Big man, get down here on Saturday morning, 10.30.' Like McGarry, he could never bring himself to address me by name.

I turned up for the interview in style. My friend, former Wolves goalkeeper Malcolm Finlayson, drove me to the ground in his Rolls-Royce. The Press were there and I was on time. Until 10.42 am I was kept waiting in the corridor. One of the directors, Wilfred Sproson, had not arrived. No courtesy was extended to me and I felt like a spare part, standing there in the corridor, waiting to be called to the inner sanctum. When I entered, Harry Marshall was at the top of the table, flanked by Malcolm Goody, George Clarke and Wilfred Sproson. Gerry Divine, a director who had once told me that if they had each been told to put £5,000 into the club he would have to resign, was not in attendance. I was told he was on holiday.

The chairman greeted me formally and said, 'We've got your file here.' This made me feel like a criminal. My file? Why did they want a file on me? I had played for Wolves from 1967 to 1975 and they were well aware of my PFA record. It was not as if I were an unfamiliar figure at Molineux.

Barely had the chairman started to speak, I realised the whole interview was nothing more than a charade. As I had read in the morning papers, John Barnwell had stated that he would have his feet behind a First Division club desk on Monday morning. A lot of people say you should not believe all you read in the newspapers, but I believed this. It rang true. I knew before I went to the ground that it was all cut-and-dried, but I had to go through the motions if only to show up the false pretences of the board. If I had backed out of it after learning of John Barnwell's appointment in advance of the official notification, the board could have said that I had disqualified myself. I was not going to give them that satisfaction.

I would rather Harry Marshall had said to me, 'I'm sorry, but your application came too late. The job is taken.' Instead, the charade was played out for twenty minutes. At one stage, I was asked how much I would want to manage the club and I replied, 'What do you think it is worth?' The interview, if that is what it was, was interrupted by the secretary, Phil Shaw, coming in to remind Mr Sproson, who had arrived late, that the coach going to Stoke, where Wolves Reserves were playing, would be leaving at 11 am. (It is customary for directors to take turns to accompany the reserves at away games). I remarked that if Mr Sproson was in a hurry to catch the coach, I did not want to delay him.

From the start of the so-called interview, one of the directors, George Clarke, kept looking over my shoulder at the wall clock behind me.

It was all disconcerting, but on reflection, an enlightening experience. It confirmed my belief that boards of directors do not know how to handle the affairs of their clubs in ways which honour the true interests of those connected with it.

I was the central figure in a farce. They could have told me I was not wanted, that they had already appointed a new manager, but they insisted on going through the shallow motions of a spurious interview and even then, only the chairman spoke to me. The other directors had no questions to ask. The object was apparently to appease supporters who had pressed for me to be offered the job. Supporters are not easily duped. They knew too that the interview was a pretence, because that morning John Barnwell had said in a radio interview that he expected to have his feet behind the desk of a First Division club on Monday – and Wolves were the only First Division club at the time with a vacancy. Some supporters wrote to the local paper, the Express and Star, demanding to know why I had been interviewed for a position already allocated. There was no reply from the club. What could they say, except admit that they had set up the interview as a façade? At least, I had kept faith with supporters. I only wish the directors had had the decency to keep faith with me, instead of trifling with my deep and lasting affection for Wolves. For the record, John Barnwell was appointed manager on the previous Thursday, two days before my 'interview'.

Although none of the directors said so, I had a strong feeling that they held against me my leadership of the PFA in its campaign for players' freedom of contract, Wolves being one of the Midlands 'consortium' which blocked the proposals and were instrumental in diluting them, until what we got was only a watered-down version.

None of the other directors asked me a question. I had the impression that they were in attendance just to make up numbers for the game of charades. Had they questioned me about my ideas for running a football club, I would have set out my ideas for a multi-sports redevelopment. I gain no satisfaction from thinking what I might have said and done, given the authority, when on 30 December 1980, Harry Marshall warned his staff that there was no more money available and £100,000 had already been lost on gate receipts since the start of the season, compared with attendances the previous season.

John Barnwell followed up this warning by saying he would have to prune his playing staff to get new players. 'Feeling sure that things will work out in the end,' as he put it, looked to me and other supporters as nothing more than whistling in the dark.

The pity of it all is that as chairman of the PFA I and secretary Cliff Lloyd had warned, on numerous occasions, that clubs were on a disaster course and had to change direction. But the very initials PFA often signifies something equivalent to the PLO for some directors and some managers.

Throughout my involvement in football I have experienced hostility and suspicion among them towards anyone representing the interests of the PFA, particularly club delegates, as if the association were actively engaged in a conspiracy to undermine their authority. They seem to think that the PFA is dedicated to player-power, whereas its only concern is the improvement of players' working conditions, their welfare and their security.

It reminded of Matt Gillies who said to me, when I was appointed to the PFA committee during my two seasons with Leicester City, 'We want no dressing room lawyers here.'

When I left the PFA as chairman, I advised that they should continue to pursue freedom of contract, until no fee has to be paid at the end of a player's contract. Pressure has to be brought to affect changes of attitude. Clubs and their directors do not welcome change and for this reason they remain suspicious of moves by the PFA to get better conditions for players. I believe the PFA ought to run a magazine or journal to keep members more fully and quickly informed of what is happening in the game, but I have not the slightest doubt that many managers and directors would condemn it, without even reading it, as a radical, trouble-making journal run by revolutionaries. I believe that the PFA should have a full-time president, the position renewed every three to five years. The president would be the spokesman and a figurehead for players, putting them on a par with the FL and FA (my only fear was that if anything happened to Cliff Lloyd there would be no one capable of looking after the PFA affairs until someone was groomed to take over).

Put this to directors and managers, along with proposals that all players should have pension schemes, like them and the staff at football grounds, and they react as if players are getting beyond themselves. We must keep plugging away until they accept what at present they disfavour or condemn. Twenty-five years ago six chairmen of Midlands football clubs were asked if they would spend £25,000 on floodlights at their grounds. Five said, 'No, a waste of money. Better to spend the money on new players.' Now, no self-respecting football club would be without floodlights. The most memorable matches at Molineux were played under them in the 1950s.

Battering one's head against boardroom doors can leave one with a nasty headache, but sometimes there is no alternative if progress is to be made. I can only conclude that Wolves directors regard me as a human battering ram come to shatter the foundations of their establishment, when I ponder possible reasons for their rejection of my application for shares and their refusal to allow copies of my book, Derek Dougan's Doog, about my Molineux career, to be sold at the club shop. Nor would they allow it to be advertised in their club programme. When I attend matches at Molineux – since I retired, I have had the opportunity of sitting in the visiting directors' box as a guest of the opposition – fans look up and shout, 'Hey, Doog, why are you always in the visitors' box?' and I say, 'Ask Harry Marshall.'

At the Wolves AGM in August 1976, which I attended by proxy, I was forbidden to contribute to the discussions, when all I wanted to do was make a constructive remark. In the early part of the 1980–81 season a Wolverhampton businessman, wishing to show his appreciation of my efforts for Wolves as a player, offered to me five shares. The transfer application went before the board and although the voting was three to two in favour, the chairman's decision against was decisive. No explanation or reason for this rejection was made. The decision was taken at a board meeting on 17 December 1980 but it was not until three week later that I was informed. Mr Marshall told the Press that he had been instructed by solicitors not to give a reason. I asked, through the Press, why other former Wolves players such as Malcolm Finlayson and Jimmy Mullen, should be able to buy shares and yet I should be turned down. No answer from the chairman was forthcoming.

Another example of the undemocratic process occurred

when Malcolm Finlayson, a successful businessman in the Wolverhampton area, sought membership of the board at Molineux. He had the support of most shareholders. Jack Taylor, the former international referee who was a master butcher in Wolverhampton, proposed Malcolm Goody, a nomination endorsed by Jimmy Mullen. The vote was 48 to 33 in Malcolm Finlayson's favour, whereupon someone jumped and demanded a poll vote, which meant that Harry Marshall's shares alone defeated him and the majority of shareholders.

The wishes of shareholders were rebuffed. Block shares held by the chairman were used to give a directorship to someone who had lost the shareholders' vote. The closed shop in football is more rigorous than that applied by unions on the shopfloor.

Jack Taylor's proposition in favour of Malcolm Goody did not influence my attitude towards him. I suggested to the PFA management that he should be given the merit award for his service to the game at our annual PFA awards night on 13 March 1977. Today, I regret that his reputation as a world class referee and his talents should be put to no greater use than fund raising and presenting lottery prizes at Molineux. He should have been made the referees' supremo in the United Kingdom. Referees, it seems, are their own worst enemies. They fail to explore the skill of the best among them and after enforced premature retirement are content to see men of international standing, lapse into obscurity. They ought to set up their own autonomous organisation free of the FA and FL and raise their standards, under the guidance of such a man as Jack Taylor.

For the record, I strongly criticised the FA for its decision not to appoint him referees' supremo. It was a short-sighted decision. Whatever happened to the supremo they appointed? I must confess I cannot even recall his name and for all I know he has gone into limbo. At least, we never hear of him. I read the sports columns avidly and I never come across any report of what the referees' supremo is doing or saying. Managers, secretaries and referees should all have their own autonomous organisations, enjoying equal status with the FA and FL.

Eight

All that players want – no matter what the cynics claim – is the opportunity to play regularly in the first team, whether it is the First, Second, Third or Fourth Division and the opportunity to fulfil their potential to the highest possible level. If they happen to be well paid besides that – such as £1,000 a week for Aston Villa players while on top of the First Division – then that is an additional bonus. Unfortunately managers have indoctrinated club chairmen and directors to believe unthinkingly that footballers are selfish. The only people who are selfish, in my opinion, are managers who can sign five-year contracts and 10-year contracts and walk out before a contract is a quarter of the way through, leaving their respective clubs to haggle over compensation. There is often a lot of acrimony involving managerial changes, as we saw over the John Bond and Malcolm Allison situation, which worked against the interest of the game. To help restore this the Managers' and Secretaries' Association should be split. I don't believe that the secretaries play an important role. They should have their own organisation. Managers, coaches and trainers should be separate. A managers' association should be like the British Medical Council, demanding high standards of behaviour and discipline, penalising breaches of the rules and bringing members to task when they bring the association into disrepute, the Tommy Docherty case being a good example. If their organisation is strong enough, and has teeth, it should be able to chastise its own members. On the other hand it should protect its members so that when a manager is being sacked his position should not be filled until the outgoing manager gets his entitlements from his contract. Under present conditions a manager's life is insecure. This insecurity from the management drifts into the coaching, on to the training side and inevitably drifts through to the players. Many footballers go on to the pitch reflecting the insecurity stemming from the chairman and his board of directors right through to the management, the training staff, the players and to the apprentices. Footballers can lack confidence simply through the way football is run under the present administration, only a change of approach and direction can alter this, which is why I wanted to take over a football club. I would have said, 'Give me five years and if I can't do it the way it should be done, the way I think is right, then I will surrender to the next person, or the next team of people.' At least the improvements I would initiate in a five-year period would be a starting point, providing a footing and strong foundations. They could see what I was trying to do and they might be better equipped, with more talent and perhaps greater gifts than myself. We should be tackling these negative areas now, in a positive way. First, we have to sweep away old vested interests and get rid of the cliques that run football clubs as private clubs, serving the egocentric interests of the few against the wider interests of the many.

It is appalling that people as eminent as Stan Cullis, Bill Shankly and Bill Nicholson are not playing important roles in the administration of the game and helping to implement new legislation. As managers, they were pre-eminent and their views were always sought by interviewers. What they said carried weight, because they had tremendous success, experience, insight, sense of judgment and ability. Then, when they were no longer managers, the football world seemed to lose interest in them. They were allowed to go to pasture, while anonymous men behind the scenes continued to make the decisions – or failed to make any decisions at all – without the guidance and advice of those who have made major contributions to the game.

I would like to see a consortium of people such as Cullis, 'Shanks' and football men of their calibre holding a seminar to discuss ways to improve the game, a sort of football Brains Trust. Can anyone doubt that they could make useful and important suggestions, born of their long experience? They have learned from their experience and it is appalling that they should not be in a collective position to pass on their knowledge, instead of only being called on occasionally to contribute their views in radio or TV interviews and sometimes write columns in the Press. They should be brought inside the game, not left outside. I would like to know, for instance, their ideas on how to make the game more exciting. One idea which occurs to me – and their own views would be interesting – is to scrap the present points system and replace it with a point for every goal. There would be no time wasting and 'shutting up shop' after grabbing a single goal. We would have all-out attacking football. We have to keep spectators interested and eager to follow the game.

All too often they are driven away by negative tactics and when a team is reduced to playing out the season around the middle of the table, after being knocked out of cup competitions, interest and support can dwindle. There must not be a lull in the excitement, which is why I suggest four up and down in the first three divisions and two up and down from each of a newly formed fourth division, north and south.

In substituting points for goals instead of for wins and draws, teams would be encouraged to be positive. The system would not produce too much variance at the top of the table from what it is under the present system. At the end of a season it is possible that more than four clubs, under a point-for-goal system, would be at the bottom with the same number of points. Which four then would be relegated? In those circumstances, we could have eliminating matches. Whoever wins, stays up. If there were two clubs occupying the fourth position at the top below the First Division, promotion would be decided on a home and away basis. This is what I would prefer, as the fairest means of deciding the issue. But if the respective clubs thought differently, they could reach a decision by a single game on a neutral ground.

Among other suggestions in making the game more exciting I have urged doing away with the so-called 'professional foul' and introducing a direct shot at goal with no wall, from outside the box. This would put the emphasis on positive play and deter defenders from resorting to wild tactics or irresponsible action on the pitch. I don't subscribe to the theory that the behaviour of players on the pitch influences behaviour on the terraces, but penalising the professional foul would eradicate this particular point. The advantage rule should be applied in the strictest sense of the word. I have seen too many cases where the advantage should have been played but the referee has been more interested in stopping the game, cautioning a player or having a word with him when it is not necessary. The referee could let play go on and if he wanted to take the player's number, he knows the player and could have a word with him a few seconds after the incident. If the ball is kept going there is less time for players to react. The same applies to spectators. The more one keeps the ball going the better for all concerned.

Last, but not least, I would like to see the offside rule kicked out of the game. It is negative, destructive, frustrating and antiquated. It perpetuates boring, defensive, dull tactics. I spent almost twenty years as a front player trying to overcome the offside rule, which creates unadventurous football. There are many teams whose coaches and managers cannot think beyond the offside rule and they deploy their tactics around it. We need aggressive thinking and adventurous football at international level or domestic level. The offside rule is a hindrance and infuriates players and spectators alike. The Americans have gone a little way towards dispensing with it. We should have taken these leads years ago. It is not too late. The ills we talk about in modern football can be overcome with thought and consideration. Rather than make radical changes at the end of the season, towards the end of the 1980–81 season, I would prefer the legislators and everyone concerned, including the PFA to open up the recommendations made by the Chester Committee in 1968 and go back to the Government and say, 'We are prepared to implement all of the recommendations in this report and we want to set up a Football Levy Board to bring much needed finance into the game.' Consider the amount of money the Treasury takes out of football, football deserves the same consideration that professional horse racing gets. They are on their way to getting almost £20 million out of gambling. Football deserves the same consideration.

I would stipulate that money should not be given to football in an *ad hoc* way because we have seen how the irresponsibility of football clubs, administrators and legislators can undermine progress. If they had more money coming in and were not accountable for the way it is spent they would fritter it away in transfer deals and we would see the escalation again of transfer fees. I would like the PFA to stick to their guns as they did before

1978, and say, 'If there is new money to be found, then at the end of contracts footballers should be free. All the money coming into the game should be spent to give better facilities and provide improved amenities for spectators.' With money coming from the Government and properly administered, clubs could get together with local authorities to spend the money on utilising clubs in the interests of the entire community. It is ludicrous that football grounds are open about 25 times, officially, throughout the year. Considering all the rates and rents and expenses to maintain a club opening 25 times a year is financially foolish. Clubs think it is their God-given right to expect spectators to come down in all sorts of weather conditions to support them. This attitude is no longer acceptable. As people are becoming more sophisticated and are querying everything, they say, 'What are we getting for supporting the club?' It may be that all they are getting is abused. They don't get much consideration over important matches, tickets for cup matches. A bad taste is left in the mouths of many spectators, whose team has been successful in the League Cup or in the FA Cup and when it comes to a big game, they are not considered at all. The directors and management from the higher divisions get an abundance of tickets, but the poor old spectator who has supported his team for many years, feels left out of it. If money were spent not on expensive players but on taking kids off the streets and giving them the opportunity to spend their time enjoying other sports the community at large would say, 'Look what the club is doing for us.' All the fund raising activities and the attendances would increase because people *en masse* would feel involved, instead of being treated, as they are at present, as encumbrances. The number of people who support football matches in many cases is less than five per cent of the population of a town, and for big teams such as Liverpool and Manchester United, it is even less than 10 per cent. They are not drawing on many people. The big teams get great support from outside their areas because the teams in their areas are not meeting the aspirations of the young spectators. In the event of TV, this is where Liverpool, Manchester United and Nottingham Forest, outside their own particular localities, are drawing a lot of supporters simply because of the introduction and sophistication of TV. I don't believe that all of these ideas I have outlined are radical, I believe they are fundamentally very important indeed. We have lost our way, not that I have a crystal ball and I look into it to solve all of the problems facing the football industry. The administrators, managers and secretaries have been actively involved with the reports over the last 15 years, and if they had acted on them football today would not be facing recurring and worsening crises. We would have tapped our resources to bring more money into the game from the Government, an awful lot of money, bearing in mind that TV, the pools and all the percentages of League matches and Cup matches from TV doesn't even add up to half of this a year. It could be a tremendous windfall, enabling all clubs to prepare not only for the rest of the century but for the 21st century.

The FA and FL should listen more to the PFA because they (the PFA) have greater contact with the players than the other two bodies. If support falls off further in football the FA and the FL will find it more difficult to survive. The FA could not survive without the professional side of the industry, because of all the money derived from the FA Cup final, and the FA Cup matches and international matches. A considerable sum administers all the expenses from Lancaster Gate, and keeps the FA alive. It also maintains Association Football at school level. A fall-off in support, affecting revenue will have an adverse effect in the years to come. We shall be robbed of future class players. If we don't have the finance to funnel back to the grass roots, then the grass roots will wither and die. We shall have a barren period.

The Chester Committee was aware of the football bodies' failure to capitalise on the experience and wisdom of ex-players. This failure, or rather refusal, goes back to the times when the average player was not expected to think for himself. In fact, directors and managers assumed he had no constructive thoughts worth considering and all he had to do was get on with the game and leave the thinking to his superiors. In this respect the footballer was in the same league as the private soldier, 'scum of the earth'. As long as he did what he was told and obeyed the orders of the day, no one had anything to worry about it.

The game's administrators absorbed this attitude as a natural law of football life and in spite of the enormous social changes which have occurred in the post war world, their own thinking remains locked in a time-machine. They cannot, or will not, accept the fact that many footballers have minds of their own, are capable of constructive thought, can express themselves and would be willing, given the opportunity, to put their experience to practical use within the game after their playing careers have finished. Management or coaching is all they can hope for under a system which discriminates against them in higher office.

In recommending regional stadiums and multi-sports centres, the Chester Report urged that the FA should make greater use of experts on particular committees and enquiries. 'Providing they are in a minority and are used for matters on which their expertise gives them a special standing, there is no danger to the representative and democratic character of the Association's institutions. We have in mind former professional players, experienced managers, coaches and even management experts. Few, if any, of these are likely to find their way onto the Association's committees by the present process of selection.'

The Association's rule prohibiting or limiting the participation of former or current professional players in the game's administration, was condemned by the Chester Committee as out-of-date. Article 40 of the Articles of Association states, 'No professional player, except by consent of the Council, shall be qualified to become or to continue a Member of the Council.' Rule 31 reads: 'No professional player or apprentice, nor a professional reinstated after April 30th 1924, shall be allowed to serve on the Council of this Association, or be a shareholder in it. He shall not serve on the Committee or any other association, League or Club or represent his own or any other association, League or Club, at any football meeting.'

'The Council may, if they think fit, exempt such person from any of the rule's restrictions if he gives notice in writing to the Secretary of the Association that he has ceased to play football or if he is playing without remuneration.'

The Chester Committee could see no reason for these general prohibitions. This discrimination against those who have earned their money by playing the game is an unjustified slur on a great many people who have much to offer to the administration of the game.

As I wrote in On the Spot, the phrase which caught my eye

was Article 14, about 'Professional Players' and the conditions of their transfer. When the player has regained his freedom a certificate of transfer, etc. may be asked for. The language means what it says. But where else at this stage is 'regaining' talked about, except as regards prisoners. It reminds one of the southern States in America before the Civil War.

At the core of all this is a traditional attitude towards professionalism and amateurism, as though there is a great divide betwen the two; on one side, those who play a game for money and on the other, the purists who play the game for its own sake. Some people are unable to grasp the fact that a game can be played for its own sake and at the same time professionally, as a living. This was the subject of a debate in which I took part at the Cambridge Union, on 17 November 1980. I was opposing a motion regretting the passing of the amateur in sport. As I was delivering my speech, I was thinking of the present chairman of the FA, Sir Harold Thompson, and his fondness for amateurism. The English love an amateur. Here is the text of my address:

'Traditionally, the English love an amateur. It probably has its origins in puritanism, in the feeling that good, honest work is its own reward. This is the basis of charity, to which, in a sense, amateurism is linked. A social welfare worker performs a service for which he or she is paid, professionally – and that's all right. But someone who performs the same service in the name of charity, gets the honour and the plaudits, perhaps eventually an OBE or something at Buckingham Palace.

'In sport, the amateur who does what the professional does, elsewhere, is given a similar aura of respectability and admiration. At least, this is how it used to be. Professionalism and amateurism in sport took on class divisions, reflecting those of society at large. The professionals – that is, the paid sportsmen – belonged, if you like, to the class of tradesmen. They were opportunists, entrepreneurs of the field. The amateur, almost by definition, was a gentleman of leisure who saw sport in terms of relaxation, or going a degree further, as an art or craft to be practised for its own sake. So we have the Gentlemen *v* the Players. The amateur belonged to a class which did not have to dirty its hands with filthy lucre. Amateur exponents were the purists, sportsmen who felt, or were made to feel, that being paid for what they were doing would be altogether demeaning and against the spirit of sport. Or were they? The noblest amateur of them all is said to be the bearded cricketer, W. G. Grace. I have often wondered if he were half-brother to that character in an Edward Lear limerick who had a nest of birds in his elongated beard. I suspect that W. G. Grace had a nest of 'amateur contracts' in his beard, by which I mean that in spite of popular opinion, he was not above raking in a bit on the side. In fact, quite a bit.

'After a match, tucked away in the pavilion, he could stroke his beard in satisfaction with what he was getting under the table. His mother had long before noted his skill in backplay and he was true to form, on and off the pitch. His bread was buttered on both sides, so that professionalism and amateurism became the two sides of the same coin, if you will permit me to mix a metaphor, cricket was Grace's call to fame and it was his real vocation. His mother told him that cricket was his destiny.

'He wrote hints for succeeding generations, Cricketing Reminiscences and Personal Recollections – W. G.'s Little Book, 1909 – and the royalties by the way were his.

'Two years before the birth of W. G. Grace, the bowler William Clarke argued, "I want to play cricket because I like it. It is my profession and may fairly be made as lucrative as possible. Others in my position want the same as I do. The pubic is interested in good cricket and will pay to see it."

'A call to the nation, inspired by the Prince of Wales in a letter to the editor of the Daily Telegraph, resulted in a collection of £5,000 for the veritable and distinguished amateur, W. G. Grace, whose years of grace made him an exceedingly wealthy man from cricket.

'Had he announced that he was turning professional, Grace would have suffered a loss of esteem. George Santayana was right when he said that the English genius is anti-professional and that its affinities were with amateurs. So it was, in the days when Britain had an Empire and the amateur spirit, developed in the public schools, could be harnessed to administer the colonies. Amateurism flourished until the outbreak of the Great War in 1914, when amateur soldiers (Kitchener's volunteers) paraded themselves for king and country and were mown down on the Somme and at Ypres. The professionals –

the regulars – at first despised the newcomers, fresh from school, office or factory. There was a gulf between them, part military and part social, yet they did the same jobs in the trenches and died together in the mud.

'Since then, the great divide between amateur and professional has lessened and now, I believe, there is no profound difference, only an artificial barrier.

'Some old prejudices, like old soldiers, never die and take a long time to fade away. I find it dispiriting that prejudice, bound by antiquated rule books, should determine the fate of such amateurs as David Duckham, Gerald Davies and Gareth Edwards, Ian McLauglin and maybe J. P. R. Williams himself incurring the disapproval of the Rugby Union for accepting payment for books and newspaper articles. I ask you! What crime have they committed in the name of sport? In what way have they defamed the status of amateur? If they had stipulated that all royalties should go to the Union itself, or to some charity, perhaps they would have been spared the heavy handed treatment. Can rugby really afford to discard the experience of such players, when they could contribute enormously to the sport's coaching and training? The Welsh Rugby Union has made a million pounds profit plus out of the All Blacks tour, and sponsorship. Why should the players responsible for all this profit and interest not benefit themselves? Amateur status is used to disguise a hundred sins against those who participate, while their overlords reap the rewards.

'Do we really imagine that a dedicated amateur has actually desired not to be paid, not receive any emoluments, feeling that this would foul his nest? In all probability, the amateur has often been accumulating a few nest eggs, in private, I don't have to touch on the perks. Everyone knows they exist and multiply, which makes the whole amateur business a charade and hypocritical.

'The amateur often remains an amateur because he has the security of another job. After picking up his salary as, say, a bank clerk or a town hall bureaucrat, he plays his sports and collects his expenses, which can be manipulated according to the circumstances and the occasion.

'When I was a young footballer in Northern Ireland I was good enough to play, at the age of fifteen with professional players five and more years older. But because I could not sign a professional contract until I was 17, I was classified as an amateur and received 25 shillings a week expenses. At the time I was earning 7s. 6d a week as an apprenticed electrician in the shipyard. So it paid me, really, to play for expenses and it paid the club because they were getting me relatively cheaply. They would have had to pay a senior player far more, six pounds in fact was the maximum wage. This was the system. Twenty years later the professionals were still receiving £6 a week.

'Perhaps it's time I should distinguish between the amateur who is, in effect, a professional and the amateur who sprinkles divots on golf courses at weekends, the lads who run around the parks for their health, the hockey players of St Trinian's . . . These are the true amateurs, who are not pushing their skill beyond their own grades.

'There is a tendency to link them all under the misleading title of amateur, a legacy of the period when Lord Kinnaird in football, and Lord Hawke in cricket practised sport for its own sake and when it brought prestige to enhance other, more pecuniary interests. A "blue" at university helped to conceal an indifferent scholastic record, an international cap worked wonders in business. Lords and bishops knew where to put their oars!

'Even going back to the fifteenth century, we find footballers on St Catherine's day being paid fourpence by the Prior of Bicester – and in modern times that might be several hundred pounds. A St Catherine wheel of fortune you might say!

'At the beginning of the last century, Capt. Barclay Allardice announced that he would set out to walk 90 miles in 21½ hours. In the name of sport? A long distance walk for its own sake? The officer was a gentleman and an amateur – but he collected 500 gns for his feat. There was, apparently, no distinction between amateurs and professionals.

'I submit that the difference is a matter of attitude, that it is all in the mind – and the mind needs de-frosting.

'Too many double standards make a mockery of the distinction anyway. Do professional writers complain when a professional sportsman writes a book? Of course not. They don't complain that he is an amateur writer and has no right to trespass on their professional territory.

'But when an amateur sportsman writes a book, he is told by his sporting overseers that he has breached the amateur's code of practice.

'Many amateur sportsmen raise their skill to a professional level. They should not be penalised simply because they wish to retain their daily vocations. Nor should the professionals worry about amateurs beating them at their own games.

'As I said, it is largely a matter of attitude and prejudice, well summed up by Robert Graves in a passage from one of his books. "For a woman to have a liaison is almost always pardonable and occasionally, when the lover chosen is sufficiently distinguished, even admired. But in love as in sport the amateur status must be strictly maintained."

'For whose benefit? Well I leave the question open, and conclude with another quotation, this from G. K. Chesterton, "The artistic temperament is a disease that afflicts amateurs." I will go one better and say that the amateur temperament is a malaise that afflicts those who wish to maintain old class divisions, and who have a vested interest in keeping the amateur in a cubby-hole, exploiting his talents while denying him freedom of expression. The amateur is often no more than a bondsman. . . . In the interests of an egalitarian society and democratic principle, I welcome not only the blurring of the line between professional and amateur, but the eradication of it – in the interest of sport, for its own sake and those who play it, at whatever level.

'We slip too easily into pre-conditioned attitudes generated by the very words. *Amateur* takes on a connotation of being low grade, down market and poor quality. *Professional* sounds highly efficient, sophisticated and capable. Thus, the amateur on the stage ranks far below the professional, even when Peter O'Toole's Macbeth, on an amateur stage would be regarded as "typical" and a highly proficient amateur performance fails to gain the recognition it deserves.

'Many amateur sports people have proved themselves the equals or the superiors of professionals – and even in our cover-up society it is no secret that they do enjoy financial rewards, channelled to offset allegations of professionalism. It is only when the amateurs break their cover and accept fees for books and articles, that the rule books are thrown at them.

'The passing of the amateur in sport means the true and open *acceptance* of the amateur in sport, an end to all the cloak-and-dagger manœuvres. Let us get on with the game – and put a stop to the *gamesmanship*, that divides *amateurs* and *professionals* and only perpetuates an obsolete class system.'

Nine

People cannot elect themselves to the council of the FA or to the various management bodies. They have to receive general support. The Chester report recommended that the rules prohibiting or limiting the participation of former or current professional players in the administration of the game, should be abolished. Of course they have not all been abolished. This is but one of the many far-sighted recommendations made in the report to be noted, casually discussed and then put to one side. Norman Chester received a knighthood for the report and I believe he is a regular attender at football matches especially at Oxford. It must be galling for him to know that after 13 years his detailed and visionary report, which could have saved football from the crises it now faces, continues to collect dust in the pigeon-holes where so many reports are consigned. He must feel like Bernard Shaw, who on a visit to the United States, in the early 1930s, was asked about his views of the Depression. Tetchily, he replied, 'I've been here before, you know. I told you what to do then, and you haven't done it. So why do you ask me again?'

Sir Norman Chester has not been asked to repeat or revise his report. There would be no need to re-write it. The report is as valid today – more so – than when it was produced. All that needs to be done is to re-open the 135 pages and act on the recommendations. The blueprint is there in the green-backed report, entitled 'Report of the Committee on Football', published by Her Majesty's Stationery Office, for the Department of Education and Science.

The final plaintive paragraph reads, 'We hope that the very modesty of our proposal (a levy board) will charm the Government and Parliament into giving general support to the necessary legislation.' It didn't. The Government and the football authorities have remained obdurate in their resistance to change. Although the game is beleaguered, staggering from one crisis to another, lurching out of control and losing support, those in charge behave like Captain Queeg in The Caine Mutiny, bent on a course that is clearly destructive and using their powers of command to keep what they claim is a set, direct course from which there must be no wavering. Even when their minions are franctically signalling the iceberg in their path or warning of approaching gales, they cannot appreciate the need for changing the direction they have maintained for more than a century. Enclosed in their boardrooms and out of immediate contact with supporters, whom they hardly notice when they take their seats in the directors' boxes, chairmen and directors, like the administrations in Lancaster Gate and at Lytham St Anne's, are insulated from reality. But the reality confronts them in the statement of accounts. Simple arithmetic should convince them that they cannot continue to pay their way from gate receipts, when these are toppling, in spite of higher admission charges. Nor can they rely on funds from lotteries and sponsorship. Every little helps but it is not enough. Massive injections of cash are needed and these can only come from a government levy board, from sponsorship schemes and by redeveloping grounds for families to enjoy a diversity of entertainment and recreation, with football as the nub.

Football began as a game for the ordinary people and became the national sport. It has been taken over by cliques and bureaucrats. The time has come to return the game to the people, without whose involvement and co-operation it will not survive, except at grass root level on recreation grounds and on school playing fields. Although professional football is an institution, it has no divine right of survival, any more than the music hall had – and look what happened to the greatest form of entertainment the world has known, the cinema! Football can go the same way, one club following another into oblivion. This need not be. The means to re-establish the game and make it permanently secure, are available. All that is required is the vision to utilise resources and the willingness to alter the administrative structure, which acts as a palsied hand on a game ill served by those who control it. I am not a lone voice crying in a football wilderness. I am only reflecting and enlarging on the inner thoughts and feelings of thousands of supporters and the official recommendations of those who have compiled successive reports on the game over the past 15 years. We have a choice – to re-develop football grounds as multi-sports centres and watch them prosper or allow grounds to stagnate into wastelands. All that most of them get apart from re-seeding and re-turfing is a new coat of paint at the end of a season.

Coventry and Aston Villa have developed training areas and the Sky Blues have opened the Sky Blue Connection, a sports centre much admired by the Duke of Edinburgh when he performed the official opening. But they have not developed their grounds as sports complexes.

It is to the football grounds that people want to go, not to sports centres detached from them. For generations they have associated themselves with football grounds and where they have broken away, it is only because the grounds no longer offer them enough diversion and not enough facilities. They would be only too pleased to return, if there was more to attract them. A sports centre associated in name with a football club will not be identified with the club. It will become autonomous and risks becoming remote. How then can it possibly help to develop and further a football club's interests?

We could even reach a point where a separate sports centre is doing better than the football club to which it is associated. It is impractical to expect a football follower to drop off his family or friends at a sports centre and then continue his journey to the ground. In one community complex, there would be a sense of unity and common sharing.

When I was invited to join the committee of the PFA and later became chairman, I had a genuine desire to help improve the welfare and conditions of my fellow players. I mention this not to claim any special virtue, which would be immodest, even for an Irishman! but to contradict an ungenerous impression that I have been motivated by self-interest. At various clubs, where I was a PFA delegate, representing the players, I found managements and directors suspicious of my activities, as if I were organising underground political cells, to subvert their authority and bring the clubs crashing over their heads. They would not or could not appreciate a simple fact that I was only trying to ease relationships between them and players in dispute and also further the interests of the clubs.

Sometimes, the suspicion was paranoiac, as at Wolves, when the management appeared to be convinced I was trying to oust them and install myself! It may appear that I am hard on the game's administrators. If so, it is not for the sake of being hard. I care about my profession. I care for the future of professional football and I see it wasting away from ignorance, neglect and downright foolishness. It is within the power of the administrators and legislators to overhaul the rules and procedures, to enable the game to prosper, within a wider social and sporting framework, but they continue to squander their assets and fail to capitalise on their resources.

We see millions of pounds spent on new stands, used no more than 25 or so times a year, dragging clubs into debt, while they struggle to pay vast amounts in interest charges on the fortunes they have borrowed. Near my home in Wolverhampton I have seen a new stand emerge, with the space below reserved for the use of the town's Polytechnic. The club will get a rent of less than £50,000 a year but they are having to pay almost £4,000 a week at time of writing in interest charges after acquiring a loan to build the stand. No provision has been made for new facilities, such as squash courts, badminton, indoor tennis, and other leisure activities; nothing for public use during the week. The redevelopment plan follows the contours of the existing ground, accommodating more than 40,000 spectators. The average gate is no more than 20,000. The days when Molineux could be packed, bursting at the seams, even several times a season, are gone. I doubt if they will return, regularly.

The club should have seized the opportunity to plan for a new age, of diversified sports and recreations, by building around a smaller perimeter, to accommodate 30,000 spectators seating at the most and incorporating in the stand a multi-sports centre with accessible car parks. The consequence of a wasteful and ill-advised development plan, started before the club had restored the successful patterns of the fifties, is that it has been postponed (that is, abandoned for the foreseeable future) because there is no money left. The new Molineux Street stand does not generate the income needed to complete other phases. How could it, when it is used only on Saturday afternoons and is never full? Where else but in football would boards of directors lay out so much money for such little return?

Like many club Wolves say they have to sell players before they can buy new players, so players are sacrificed, to help defray crippling debts. Again, it is the players who suffer, through no fault of their own, when the planners and administrators have done their worst through lack of vision and commonsense. It is not the players who get clubs into this state. Why not sell directors instead? On reflection, who would want most of them, even on free transfers?

This is why I have always pleaded the cause of the players and been angry at the injustices done to them. As one club after another in the early part of the 1980–81 season announced mounting debts, some pundits predicted that 600 players would have to be put up for transfer, or free transfers in desperate attempts by their clubs to make up the deficiencies from falling gate receipts. And where would they go, if so many clubs were on the poverty line? A vicious circle has emerged, widened by the transfer system and the unrealistic fees which have priced highly-rated players almost out of the game, or at least prevented them from going to the clubs of their choice. We see talented players condemned to playing in the reserves when through circumstances, such as change of a manager, they do not command a first team place but are prevented from leaving through being excessively priced.

Footballers are the game's pawns, to be shuffled about as managers and directors decree, with little or no regard for their feelings or their security. And yet the game depends on them, the players; they are all-important and are the least considered. Their thoughts, judgments, observations and opinions are never sought by those who would benefit from them. When they speak up for themselves they are instantly reprimanded and fined by their clubs for speaking out of turn, without permission, as if they were school children carrying tales out of class.

It was not natural for me to remain silent and it is hard to be Irish without being political. By this, I do not mean politically partisan or committed to a particular cause or party. I mean political in a wider sense, having regard to the conditions and way of life of people everywhere. Although I came to England in my teens and have since lived on the mainland, I have deep affinities with Ireland and feel that sense of guilt which occurs when someone leaves his or her native land and witnesses its problems and troubles from a distance. People's charitable instincts are often aroused by their own privileges. Having two boys in excellent mental and physical health, I was drawn years ago to helping the mentally and physically handicapped and the Mental Health Research Fund. By the same token, I have a strong desire to do all I can to help overcome the problems of Northern Ireland. Of course, better men than I have tried and failed and I do not have a magic wand to wave over the benighted province. But there is one contribution I could have made and tried to make.

My experience and reasoning tell me that people are much the same the world over. Confucius, he say . . . long ago, that it is only circumstances that divide people. In England, Irish Catholic and Protestants live next to one another without rancour. Irish Protestants and Catholics play football together, without sectarian ill-feeling. It is only in Ireland that sinister, brooding and murderous passions are enflamed. Flames can be damped down and one of the best ways to do so is by stimulating the sporting spirit.

For some years I have advocated the formation of an all-Ireland football team. There would be two obvious, far-reaching benefits. A national side, non-sectarian, would draw together the two communities and at the same time the power and prestige of Irish football would have an international base. Under the present system, neither the north nor the south has the resources to make a consistent impact in competitive international football. But there are skilled players, north and south, who together in one team could be regular contenders in the World Cup Finals and in the Nations Cup Finals.

It may not be politically possible, or even desirable, to have a united Ireland for some years to come, but a united spirit could help to relieve the tensions that pull the two communities apart. Football is an emotional game and it can absorb the emotions of an entire country. An all-Ireland side would show to the people of the north and the south and to the world, that there are common unities and goodwill can be fostered in spite of religious and political differences.

This seemed to me so self-evident, no one really had to argue the case. But someone, I felt, had to get the idea off the ground, or on to the ground, in Dublin and Belfast, by means of a trial run. My idea was to organise two matches, North *v* South, in Dublin and Belfast, and having thus established goodwill on both sides of the border, to follow up with the formation of an all-Ireland side.

An ideal opportunity to outline the scheme came when I was preparing with the Northern Ireland side to go and play against Cyprus on 14 February 1973. At the team's hotel in London, before departure, I spoke to Billy Drennan, the secretary of the Irish FA and Harry Cavan, the president. I said it would be a marvellous opportunity to establish a sense of calm between the communities. The first venue could be decided by the toss of a coin. I suggested that the proceeds, boosted by live TV coverage, could go towards refurbishing the floodlights at Windsor Park and to Mary Peters' appeal for funds for a tartan track for aspiring and deprived atheletes. At the end of the 1972 close season when Northern Ireland beat England one—nil at Wembley in the home championship, security officials in Belfast told me that the streets were practically deserted and all was peaceful, because people were indoors watching the highlights on TV and listening to the radio commentary. The whole of Ireland, north and south would be watching the two games on TV and this could only result in mass goodwill. I said it would be a tremendous gesture, encouraging people to forget the past and concentrate on the future, something which neither the Pope nor King Billy had been able to do.

Harry Cavan listened to me and said, 'A good idea, but the timing is not right.' I was astonished. What did he mean by the timing not being right? It was because of the tension that the timing was right. I went away disappointed by the negative response.

After the match in Cyprus I was dropped from the Northern Ireland side. I never played again for my country. This could not have been through loss of form. Fourteen months later I played for Wolves against Manchester City at Wembley in the League Cup Final, and I played in the First Division for two more years, while the selectors called on players who could not even hold first team places in lower League sides. I had been on my way to getting my fiftieth international cap, which would have admitted me to the elite company of Pat Jennings, Billy

Bingham, Jimmy McIlroy, Danny Blanchflower and Terry Neill.

It is normally the custom on reaching a fiftieth international appearance to have a presentation, recipients are usually given gold watches. Instead of being given the opportunity to reach the 50 mark, I found the stop-watch was brought out and my time was up.

It was common knowledge over the years that Terry Neill, the former Irish manager, and I did not get along too well. During Billy Bingham's management there was friction between Terry Neill and me off the pitch. On the pitch, even sworn enemies tend to forget their differences in the common cause. Neill was manager at the time of the game in Cyprus and he was close to Harry Cavan, which did not go unnoticed by members of the squad. It is possible that Harry Cavan discussed my idea with the manager and decided not to recommend it. It would not have been easy for me to approach Terry Neill on the matter, because I never found him easily approachable. He was never seen mixing much with the players after a match. When we relaxed, he was elsewhere. I have no proof, but I am convinced that my exclusion from the side was a deliberate act of policy in response to my feelings about an all-Ireland side. I believe that bigotry and prejudice stopped me from making a practical contribution to the cause of Irish football.

In view of the dislike of Terry Neill by some members of the squad, I could have made his task as manager difficult, but I didn't. My attitude, as with the rest of the lads, was that we were 'doing it' for Northern Ireland and nothing else really mattered.

The Irish have an aggressive team spirit, but it has not been harnessed as it should for the entire country. I might not have been selected for an all-Irish international side at the time, but there were plenty of top-class players who could have made a big impression on the football world, such as George Best, Pat Jennings, Alan Hunter, Jimmy Nicholson, Johnny Giles, Steve Heighway, Don Givens, to name but a few. If there had been an all-Ireland side, I am sure that George Best would not have gone off the rails. His erratic behaviour was sometimes caused by frustration. Here was a brilliant player, an absolute genius, without the international showcase he needed. Had he been born English, he would have had no problem. In the England side, he would have excited the world. In a Northern Ireland jersey, he was rarely seen on a world stage. Fortified by regular international appearances in Cup competitions around the world, his ambitions would have been fulfilled and his skill given the international recognition it merited. Restricted by nationality, he remained an outsider, never able to reach the centre of the top international footballing events. It was like an actor such as John Gielgud being denied the National Theatre stage and forced to appear on the Fringe with a small workshop company. I am sure this tipped the balance in Best's personality and finally drove him away and then back into showbiz soccer in the United States, where at least he has found lucrative financial rewards. The Press in Britain gave him a bad time, playing up his unpredictable behaviour as if he were Peck's Bad Boy and pursuing him everywhere. His private life was sensationalised and he was crucified unfairly after the joy he gave to us all and to the critics who were agog at this talent even when they were condemning his behaviour.

'Crucified' is not too strong a word. It was a custom in the ancient world to make a living sacrifice of those whom the gods had granted special favours. They were honoured, feted and all their whims indulged, until the time came for a blood sacrifice to appease the gods. George Best was a latter-day version of this ritual. He had special gifts. It was as if he had been singled out by the fates to shine above his fellow players, to inhabit an honoured place in the football world reserved for one exceptional star every generation. Fame and fortune were granted to him and then, in the tradition of moralistic myths, the king was made victim; the chosen favourite was sacrificed on the altar of public fan worship.

There has never been a more electrifying player in the English League. I recall Sir Matt Busby recalling the trepidation of a rival supporter, who seeing that Best had the ball, murmured, 'Oh, God, he's got the ball. What's he going to do now?' That was the point. One never could be sure what he would do but whatever he did, he did with style, grace and brilliance. When comes such another? I grieve for the loss his departure meant for creative, intuitive football on the English scene. I lament the lost joys. I am proud to have played alongside him in the

Northern Ireland side, but I knew it was not enough for him, wearing a Northern Ireland jersey. He should have had the world at his feet in an all-Ireland jersey and instead he became a notoriety, transferred from the sports pages to the gossip columns. I could not say to him, in the words of the Irish poet, W. B. Yeats, 'Grow old along with me, the best is yet to be.' The best years of his life were what might have been ...

For my own part, I had compensations, such as passing the immortal Peter Doherty's record and becoming the first Irish player in the English League to score 200 league goals. I was also the longest serving post-war chairman of the PFA. I did not lack honours, but I deeply regret that an all-Ireland side remains only an idea, prevented from coming into being by vested interests. An impartial cynic said to me, when I mentioned the idea, 'That would mean one president, instead of two, wouldn't it?' He went on, 'and one manager instead of two. One set of selectors instead of two ... one trainer instead of two.' Who would agree to step down? There's the rub. A number of officials and hangers on would be deprived of their social perks. Their travel arrangements would be curtailed. I remember being with the Irish party for a Nations Cup match in Seville, some ten years ago. There were 14 players in the party of nearly 40. You see what I mean? Harry Cavan said the timing was wrong. I discovered after the event that he did his best to cancel the friendly fixture between an Irish side and Brazil, in Dublin. The match came about in a fortuitous way. I had a phone call from Johnny Giles, saying that his brother-in-law, Louis Kilcoyne, wanted to see me. Louis came to my home and announced that he was going to Brazil to get the national team to play in Dublin during a world tour. I said, 'You're joking.' I thought Brazil must be where the 'nuts' go to, not just where they come from! But his enthusiasm and determination impressed me and I promised to throw in my lot in with him. 'If you get Brazil I'll help get the players from the north.' He set up the Brazilians and the arrangements were made for the match on 4 July 1973, Independence Day, but it had to be brought forward a day because of flying arrangements.

Louis got them to play for Unicef, raising funds from TV coverage for this worthy children's charity. The Brazilians did not get a fee, only expenses. In spite of persistent rain all day, the game was attended by over 30,000 spectators and was shown live on television. I was honoured and thrilled to be in the Irish side and to give the world masters a close contest. They won 4—3. People from the North of Ireland travelled south to see the game, which was a major sporting and social event. If any had worries about security, they were soon dispelled. There was no trouble and no one asked about religious or political associations. At the start of the 1973–74 season, at the Park Hall hotel, Wolverhampton, I was in conversation with Sir Stanley Rous the former president of FIFA. Over dinner he informed me that Harry Cavan had done his best to stop us playing an all-Ireland side. He successfully intervened to stop us wearing the Irish green colours of the national side, and we had to call ourselves a Shamrock Rovers select eleven. He had, apparently, sent telegrams to get the match put off, claiming it was too much of a risk. He did not attend the game, evidently overlooking the fact that the troubles were in the north, not in the south. I told Sir Stanley it had been a tremendous success.

The match between Shamrock Rovers select eleven and Brazil might have initiated an all-Ireland side, but interference behind the scenes to deprive the event of its all-Ireland connotations precluded further attempts to pursue the scheme. Goodwill has been sacrificed for the sake of narrow vested interests and old traditions, which are kept artificially alive. The social and perks circuit appears to be more important for some FAI and IFA officials and the spongers than the good of the game. An all-Ireland side, reaching the finals of the World Cup and the Nations Cup would bring a considerable amount of money into the game, to benefit the small clubs and the grass roots struggling for existence on both sides of the border. Apart from wasting its own talented individualists, Irish football is today wasting itself. Some of its administrators have done well out of the game, socially. I only wish Irish football had done as well out of its administrators.

Ireland is too small to justify two national sides. There are not the top quality players to spread over the dividing line and achieve international distinction.

Should the people of Ireland, north and south, and the football world, need evidence to support the creation of an all-Ireland team they need look no further than the career of

George Best, whose brilliance and creative genius qualified him for international acclaim but who was driven to distraction by his frustrations and disappointments. All any sportsperson wants to do in life is to get the ultimate out of a sporting career at the highest possible level.

Ten

Wherever I look and whichever way I turn in the football world, I see British football failing to take advantage of the options open to it. It is like crowds of people, driven to the shore by a forest fire, wading into the deep water until it covers their heads, instead of walking across the wide and secure bridge built for them by competent engineers and giving, as their reason for not using the bridge, that they have not set foot on it before and so cannot be sure it is safe. The bridge to safety was built by the Chester Report and it still remains discarded.

Overall, the game is crying out for a new administrative structure, supported by a regular flow of funds from government sources in return for all the pools tax paid to the Treasury. So far successive governments have been distracted by the huge sums paid out by clubs in transfer deals. Denis Howell used to tell Cliff Lloyd and me, 'How can I, as Sports Minister, get money from the Treasury when the Chancellor sees how much money is being spent on transfer fees?'. It was a valid question. Chancellors naturally assume that football clubs are rolling in money. The truth is that most clubs are scraping money from the barrels they are rolling.

The football authorities have been telling us, from time to time, what they might do and they have done very little to put the game to rights. It is time they listened to and acted on a few constructive proposals before there is nothing left of the game for them to act on anyway.

A starting proposition is an acknowledgment of a basic condition of competitive life – that people need something to aim for, something to give them an incentive. Whatever the amateur purists say, the game is not played for its own sake. A team which did not care whether it won or lost and did not care whether it won promotion or was relegated, would soon transmit its attitude towards spectators and they would lose interest.

Of Course, the game and how it is played is important. Skill and entertainment-value cannot be minimised, but on top of the intrinsic values and virtues there has to be competition and striving for status.

For this reason I would like to increase the opportunities for non-League sides to join the League. Under the present system, most of them do not stand a chance. The old boys' network is run as a closed shop, the only true one in Britain run by employers. The *status quo* is nearly always maintained. A bottom Division club can finish at the bottom season after season and, by successful lobbying and with friends in the right places, can still get re-elected to the League, when ambitious and successful non-League sides, which have done all they can to justify entry, are kept out such as Altrincham who won the Alliance League last season and still could not get in.

It is galling for them to put their grounds in shape, raise money, increase support, top their leagues and run smack into a wall, battering their heads against it without being able even to shake the foundations. There are about seven thousand professional footballers in England, full-time and part-time, on club payrolls, and they all need hope. What hope is there for non-League players when a League side can re-apply for re-election so many times?

In my two years with Kettering Town I had ample opportunity to talk to officials and players in non-League football and I came to appreciate their concern. They wanted a new structure, giving them better opportunities to fulfil their ambitions.

I admit that some non-League clubs do not wish to enter the League and are content with part-time football. Admission to the League under the system I have outlined, would not be compulsory. If a club, winning the championship of a Premier league, did not wish to enter the Fourth Division, the next in line could do so. But I am convinced that the very thought of getting into the League would give non-League clubs the incentive to improve their grounds and overall standards.

The finishing position need not necessarily dictate entry. There are many aspiring non-League clubs, around the country, denied the fulfilment of their hopes and ambitions by the present system, which discriminates unfairly in favour of the clubs already in the Football League and militates against non-

League football. Under the system I have outlined, they would be motivated and encouraged. Further, there would be a surge of interest among supporters.

It is demoralising for a club expelled from the League, knowing that it cannot get back. Support is bound to dwindle and players lose heart. Consider the fate of Gateshead, Workington and Barrow over the past twenty years. Out of the League, they know the door is shut behind them for ever.

A club relegated to the non-League ought to be able to take stock of itself, re-charge its batteries and prepare for promotion. Another immediate benefit my scheme would have is the possibility of a newly-formed club gaining League status within a few years. We must get down to the grass roots, from which football grows.

At the same time, while reducing the number of clubs in the First Division to twenty, to help form a composite League of 100 clubs in four divisions the work load of star players in successful sides, would be eased. The reduction of four games in the First Division's League season would enable clubs to cope better with fixtures when extreme weather in the winter takes its toll. Also, there would be time to postpone a game for clubs to release international players to play for their countries.

This saving of four games would allow us to start the season at the beginning of September and finish the season by the end of April, thus providing greater breathing spells.

Why not give it a try? Nothing would be lost and there is much to be gained. Half measures are not the answer, but at present this is what we are being given.

There has been talk of Sunday football, but the moment it is proposed the traditionalists leap about protesting that it would not work. Those who never go to church claim that the churches would object. Alas for them! More than 300 years ago King James I made all clergymen read out from their pulpits from the Book of Sports which was to promote healthy sport on Sundays!

Although there are obvious drawbacks, especially for those newspapers which still publish Saturday sports editions, I believe the advantages to the game would be overwhelming. Attendances would be boosted by people who have to work on Saturday afternoon, such as shopkeepers and assistants.

Significantly, attendances at football grounds are often greater in the evenings, for mid-week matches, than on Saturdays. Why not try Sunday football as an experiment for a season? And why not bring a top League match forward to, say, Thursday evening for live television coverage. The fans are tired of snippets and of 'highlights' which are often not highlights at all, only edited fragments of a match. The clubs chosen for live coverage on a night when there are no other matches, could be guaranteed against any possible loss in attendance, by making up in payment the difference between attendance and ground capacity. Think what mass public interest there would be in a Thursday evening match on TV between Liverpool and Everton or Ipswich and Nottingham Forest.

Sadly, the football authorities are only tinkering with the game's problems instead of making bold and imaginative leaps forward. The game is stumbling between Victorian concepts and modern pressures. There is no other game which so closely reflects the changing patterns and trends of society as football. As life becomes more competitive, so does football become quicker and sharper, requiring split-second reflex actions by the players, whose training has been intensified to keep pace with pressures exerted not only by managers and trainers, but the subtle pressures of society itself. If you want a mirror image of a community, go to the local football ground and study the play.

It is futile to lament the passing of 'the old styles' when teams fielded five in attack, three half-backs and two full backs. In its day, the style reflected the times. Today, though there is often too much emphasis on defence, even this is revealing. It reflects hesitancy and fear of failure, which are characteristics of any competitive society.

The irony is that while the game has kept pace with the age on the pitch, it has languished in Victoriana in the perimeter. Most grounds remain monuments to the past, virtual tombs of a footballing way of life which has no relevancy to the needs of today. Players have progressed while those in power over them, the legislators and administrators, have preserved the old *status quo* and have only conceded progressive changes when they have been forced upon them. Why should it have taken more than three years for the PFA to negotiate with the football authorities for a watered down version of freedom of contract for players, when an immediate acceptance of it in principle would have brought the game into line with other professions? And then, after protracted negotiations, why should a number of club chairmen refuse to accept a multiplying factor to determine transfer fees? Why should freedom of contract be watered down instead of being granted in full?

The answer is painfully obvious, that the hierarchy fears any encroachment on its traditional plutocratic authority. Concessions made here and there are intended only to keep 'the radicals' quiet. Sometimes the plutocrats – club chairmen – get together and 'look busy', like the parish priest when the bishop told him that Christ was returning. Their conference at Solihull was given a lot of Press coverage and the chairmen gave an impression that they were anxious to overhaul the game to make it more exciting and win back missing spectators. Again, they only trifled with the issues and failed to deal with the fundamental structure of the game, where the re-building has to begin.

On arrival at the conference, they should each have been presented with copies of the Chester Report, given the first day of the conference to read and ponder it and Monday should have been devoted to discussions on its recommendations and how to implement them. They are more crucial now than when they were proposed, thirteen years ago. I would like to say that in the Chester Report the means of reviving professional football and enabling it to prosper are staring the legislators and administrators in the face. This would not be accurate, because for strange and mysterious reasons they have averted their gaze from it. How many club chairmen have read the Chester Report? I would not be surprised if some have not even heard of it and think it is a comedy script by Charlie Chester. It ought to be a ready reference book on their desks. Until they open its pages and their own minds, football will continue to flounder and the crowds will drift away. The 1980–81 season has been a watershed, with attendances down and the worsening recession taking its toll. This should have stirred the football authorities in action, taking up the spirit of the general who said, 'My position is hopeless – I shall attack.' Sadly and tragically, they are too set in their ways, too complacent and not imaginative enough to grapple with the fundamental changes which are needed to rescue football from the doldrums that precede the grave. It would be absurd to claim that football has a death-wish, but it is suffocating under the dead hand of a system suffering from senile decay and hardening of the arteries.

Clubs throughout the League, even at the top, are merging into two sides doomed, under the present system, to playing each other to a standstill – Penury United *v* Bankrupt Rovers. The writing need not be on the wall. It can be found in my football Bible, the Chester Report, other reports on the game and in the pages of this book, in which I have tried to offer a blueprint for the game in the 1980s and show how it could be developed.

Eleven

Now is the time for reflection. As we are fond of saying in Britain, the British are never happier than when they have their backs to the wall. There is a kind of morbid delight in being down and not quite out, so that in an emergency we can rally together and having lost all the other battles, win the last, crucial one. The Battle of Britain was fought in that do-or-die spirit.

Football has its back to the wall and the wall is crumbling. The time has come for a do-or-die fighting spirit to reclaim the game. As I see it, the players themselves will have to battle it out through their organisation, the PFA, which over the years has proved it is the most enlightened, constructive and efficient of all the organisations within the game. The crucial battle on which the survival and future progress of the game depends, is for complete freedom of contract. Only when that has been attained will the administrators and legislators be forced to mend their ways and become really mindful of realities which under the present system they ignore or shrug aside, regardless of the consequences.

In earlier chapters I have emphasised faults and put forward radical proposals to improve the game at all levels. This has not been an academic exercise. Since the beginning of the 1980–81 season I have been appalled by the increasingly precarious state of the game, not so much on the playing side, for there has been a lot of quality football, but from the administrative point of view. Events at Crystal Palace, Norwich and Manchester City to name but a few clubs, have underlined the gravity of a situation which is bound to recur, time and again, unless the system is changed. We have seen how chairmen and directors can and do go their own way, wheeling and dealing, making decisions and riding roughshod over managers, players and spectators.

The Press get wind of something at boardroom level, make

inquiries, wait outside grounds, lobby administrators and are generally fobbed off with evasions, denials and contradictory statements until in the end, decisions have been made and everyone has been presented with a *fait accompli.*

Those who have the good of the game at heart and depend on it for the livelihoods, are compelled to take a back seat while directors seize the wheel and drive this way and that, up blind alleys, down dead ends, in circles and over rough ground without the slightest sense of direction or a route map. In the confusion at Selhurst Park half way through the 1980–81 season, with the chairman, Ray Bloye saying he would not, then he would, sell his shares to a Wimbledon consortium, even the team skipper, Jim Cannon, had to say, despairingly, that it was all a joke. A sick joke.

Not long before the bizarre events, Ernie Clay and Fulham were reported to be poised to take over Crystal Palace. Then Brighton and Crystal Palace were going to merge, both grounds would be sold and a new ground built near to Gatwick airport. (At least, that would have been handy for a quick flight away from football madness!)

If I had said publicly what Jim Cannon said, when I was chairman of the PFA or when I was a player at any of my six clubs, I would have been accused of bringing the game into disrepute. I have been saying it privately since I arrived in England from Ulster in 1957 and what I wrote in the first part of my autobiography, Attack! in 1969, has been totally vindicated. I wrote, 'Some directors assume that if a player is reasonably well paid he will be happy . . . some clubs do not understand the need for a happy relationship between board and players . . . a player may enjoy a lucrative contract and yet find himself the victim of a feudal system in which directors, lofty in their seats of empirical power, look on him as one of the untouchables.'

Little has changed over the intervening years. The same attitudes still prevail and I am now forced to the conclusion that only renewed, concerted efforts by the PFA's negotiating committee for complete freedom of contract, will bring about the fundamental changes needed to deliver the game to those who make it, the players and spectators.

What has happened in boardrooms and in management during the 1980–81 season has diminished the credibility of League clubs, as they are administered. We hear of players being accused of disloyalty and of supporters lacking loyalty! What of the boards of directors who are not only disloyal to them, but treat them as if they did not exist?

As attendances nose-dive, clubs should be doing all in their power to retain their confidence and enthusiasm. Instead, with a few honourable exceptions, they seem to be doing their best (or worst) to drive them away.

In view of the crises which have occurred at clubs throughout the League and the pitiful cries of directors and managers who find, after continued extravagance that they cannot afford the players they need to strengthen their teams, I regret deeply not persisting with complete freedom of contract when I led the PFA's negotiations with the Football League.

Negotiations began in January 1975 and three-and-a-half years later a compromise was reached. Only two of us on the PFA management committee, Bruce Bannister and myself, wanted to stick it out to ensure complete freedom for footballers, but persuasive arguments were put up and a balance had to be found between those clubs which treated their players well and those which wanted to maintain their feudal grip on them.

I decided it would not have been circumspect to take on the rest of the committee, so a watered-down version of freedom of contract was agreed. The alternative would have been to press ahead and take industrial action, meaning a players' strike. Directors, without financial obligations, would have had nothing to lose. The loss, in a strike, would have been borne by the players and spectators would have suffered. A strike might have broken the football-going habit of many supporters and as we know, when a habit is broken it is not always easy to restore.

At the time, I felt that this extreme course of action had to be avoided. Now, with hindsight, I believe that if I had been more resolute, whatever the immediate cost, the game would have benefited in the long run. When there seemed little or no chance of getting complete freedom for players, the PFA suggested the compromise of a multiplying factor, to determine a transfer fee on completion of contract, based on a player's age, League status and his salary. By not accepting this formula, which would have reduced transfer fees to easily manageable proportions, clubs committed themselves to their own ruination or to prolonged insolvency.

Struggling to get clear of the relegation zone, Wolves moaned that there was no money to buy new players. The fans would have put up with the old Molineux stand if they were excited by what they saw on the pitch. They did not demand a new, expensive stand and if they had known that its provision was going to leave the club without any money for team improvements, surely they would have rejected it – if they had been asked. But, of course, supporters are never asked. Decisions are made for them by directors, who claim to know best!

The transfer system can be blamed for bringing football into its present parlous state. Even the most fervent upholders of the system are now beginning to acknowledge the errors of their ways. As I have pointed out in a previous chapter, strictly speaking the system is illegal, for in law it is an offence to dispose of an asset while it is being paid for on the never-never. I know of one player who was transferred from club A to club B, went to club C and finished at club D, within a short period, before his second club had finished paying the instalments to club A. If we are to persist with the established system, there is only one way to end this ludicrous situation, by making sure that transfer fees are paid on the spot. Excessive fees, hovering around £1 million, make dramatic sports headlines, but no sense. Do directors really believe that they are doing supporters and themselves a favour when they lash out such fees on the strength of mounting bank overdrafts? It is not players' salaries that have brought many clubs to the edge of bankruptcy, as fans are often encouraged to believe, but Mad Hatter transfer fees.

If complete freedom of contract were established, directors would be jolted into reality. They would have to re-organise the administrative system, take themselves more seriously and end their dilettante approach which has bedeviled the game for so long.

There is now no latitude for continued compromise. The PFA, for the good of the game, needs to re-activate the original proposals and pursue them to a logical conclusion, even with the threat of strike action. I do not believe it would necessarily come to that, because there is now overwhelming evidence to show how complete freedom of contract would rescue the game from the transfer fees which are acting like a millstone attached to the neck of a swimmer in the deep end.

A drowning man can be expected to cling to a lifebelt, unless he is suicidal. Even the most diehard football director, confronted with the danger of a ground being swept on the rocks in swirling financial rapids, must recognise the futility of trying to build a dam with banknotes.

Clubs are bleating like lambs aware of the slaughterhouse. Directors and managers who opposed the PFA proposals, were suspicious of them and reacted as if they were nothing more than a disguised conspiracy to undermine their authority, now plead that transfer fees have escalated beyond rhyme or reason. But there is a rhyme. Here it is:

Bankruptcy is a coming.
Clubs are falling flat.
Please put a million in the transfer hat.
If you haven't got a million.
A player will do.
If you haven't got a player,
God help you!

I have never claimed special powers of perception. What I saw at clubs along my route in the Football League only led me to appreciate the law of diminishing returns. It seemed obvious to me, when I began my League career with Portsmouth, that a system which relied on horse-trading with players in no position to dictate or even influence their own careers, had within it the seeds of its own destruction.

Remoteness between directors and management, between management and players, with spectators seen and heard 'rhubarbing' on Saturday afternoons, I felt could only create strain and tension. It was like moving in a world of obsolete customs, cut off from the normal, outside world. Football has created its own rules and has behaved like a law unto itself, but at the same time it has been subjected to market forces. These forces have increased until even some of the biggest clubs are trembling. And yet directors, still convinced that the old ways are best and irrefutable, defy the laws of logic and blandly budget for anything up to £300,000 a year loss! To budget for a loss, in the hope that something will turn up, is like putting your hand into the fire in the hope that someone will provide an asbestos glove.

As a player and when I was chairman of the PFA, my admonitions were resented. It was worse when I was only a player, because players, even now, are not expected to have opinions about the game. If they do have opinions, they are not expected to voice them in public. They are expected to play the game to the best of their ability, but as soon as they express judgments, make suggestions and offer advice, managers and directors tell them to mind their own business. This instruction should really be taken literally, because they are minding their own business. Football is their business and they should be able to air their thoughts without being told they are stepping out of line.

It was my refusal to keep my mouth shut, when I thought I had something useful to say, which gave me a 'troublemaker' reputation early in my career. I could see much that was wrong with the clubs I joined and I wanted to help overcome the impediments and weaknesses. But all the time I ran into resistance, as if I were interfering in matters that should not concern me. Rather than stagnate, I moved on. Not long after I left Portsmouth, they were relegated. So were Blackburn Rovers after I had moved to Aston Villa. Villa was the only club I did not leave on my own volition. I was 'kicked out' and Villa eventually went down to the Third Division.

Peterborough, after my departure, were demoted to the Fourth Division through mal-practice and irregularities. Leicester City were relegated to the Second Division not long after I had joined Wolves.

It seems that I managed to get off sinking ships just in time.

When I finished playing for Wolves, a young girl supporter wrote to me, recalling this trend and saying, 'I hope it doesn't continue.' It did. Wolves went down the next season.

I take no pride or satisfaction in having 'escaped' before the executioner arrived. What happened was inevitable, given the way these clubs were run, with the exception of Aston Villa under Joe Mercer's management. Deficiencies at boardroom level were so obvious and management structures were so weak that decline was inevitable. No one was supposed to question the system, even when it was operating against the interests of a club. As for challenging it, whoever tried it did so at his peril.

As a player, I was in no position to do so, I could only move on, hoping for better, more enlightened administration elsewhere. It did not take long to find that the system was endemic, throughout the League.

When I was in a position to challenge the system, as chairman of the PFA, I was again resented, especially by the leading clubs of the Midlands when they 'ganged up' to resist complete freedom of contract.

Jimmy Hill, wearing his Coventry City hat, was among those against players being given absolute freedom. Twenty years ago, in his PFA hat, he campaigned for players' freedom. I would not try to diminish his magnificent achievements, especially in public relations, at Coventry City. Nor would I criticise him as a TV football presenter. Fronting Match of the Day, he is first-rate and justifiably, he has become a household name. But I challenge him to justify being party to restrictions on players in a society which regards freedom of movement as a fundamental liberty. Directors and managers take for granted their own freedom, while imposing severe restrictions on footballers. What would be the reaction in industry or commerce if a managing director or an office supervisor announced to the employees, 'I can move to another firm whenever I wish, but you can't, unless I agree, at a price.' There would be an immediate walk-out.

The Midlands clubs which stifled negotiations and almost caused them to break down, were unwilling to concede fair-mindedness and rationality by the PFA negotiating committee.

We did not state that once a proposed new system had been introduced, it could not be altered in any way. Our intention was to make provision for any change in contractual legislation to be reviewed at the end of a season, so that strengths could be built on and weaknesses overcome. There was an obvious precedent for this arrangement. Until 1973 disciplinary procedures in the game caused a great deal of heartburn. The 'courts' run by the FA were often no more than the 'kangaroo' variety. Justice was not always done, nor seen to be done. Players were resentful, feeling they would not get a fair hearing and referees were uncomfortable appearing before the disciplinary committees to give evidence.

Hearings were often reduced to fiascos, when players felt the evidence was loaded against them and that an official's word would always be preferred to theirs. Independent witnesses were not allowed, as I found to my own cost when I appeared before a committee during my time with Wolves.

After patient and constructive negotiations between the PFA and the Football Association, new procedures were worked out and implemented and these are reviewed at the end of every season. The result is that we now have a system light years ahead of that which applied until the early 1970s.

There is no reason why freedom of contract could not be introduced according to the same principles of review and re-assessment at the end of a season.

The PFA does not want to be dogmatic or autocratic. It is constituted in a democratic way and seeks only to establish systems and procedures to benefit the game and the players in the best possible way. But over the years most of its proposals and recommendations have been opposed by the football authorities. Time and again the PFA has aroused the suspicion, resentment and hostility of the FA and the Football League, through no fault of its own. Attitudes become ingrained and for too long, in the football hierarchy, there has been a lofty-minded, sometimes derisive attitude towards footballers. It is, I suppose, inevitable that this attitude should be carried forward, too, towards the association which represents the players.

Persistence will triumph in the end and the PFA will take its place of equality alongside the FA and FL. But that will not be possible until footballers have won the right to be treated like people in other professions and industries.

While they are grudgingly allowed only a limited form of freedom, they cannot enjoy equality of opportunity. It is shameful that anyone in our free society should be treated in this way, the only excuse being that football is a profession set apart from other ways of life and the 'system has to be maintained for the good of the game', a common phrase many directors and managers like to hide behind when they can find no reasonable arguments to support their prejudices.

As I have repeatedly maintained, changes will not come as a matter of course. It is no good waiting for 'a break in the weather'. Football is in a desperate state and facts speak for themselves. It is fortunate, in the 1980–81 season, that Liverpool, Ipswich and Aston Villa have concentrated attention on the First Division championship, creating excitement through close competition. Otherwise, we might have been pre-occupied with the hardships and problems of clubs lower down the table.

I don't think we have much to worry about in the state of the game, as it is played, apart from a worrying emphasis on defence by the less adventurous sides. There is plenty of good football about, but it is overshadowed by difficulties off the pitch.

In the prevailing circumstances, with distress signals going up from grounds all over the country, we might reasonably hope for club chairmen to respond by holding emergency meetings to discuss what could and should be done and then inviting representatives from all the football bodies to work with them on new schemes and ideas.

The extent of their practical concern is shown by their suggestions, such as a new points system - three points for a win, one for a draw. Under this scheme a team beaten five—four then four—three would collect no points, whereas a team which won one-nil would get three points.

Everyone - well, nearly everyone; I'm not sure about all the chairmen and directors - agrees that football needs to be made more exciting and competitive, to counteract the emphasis on defence which has followed the virtual extinction of the star-individualist-cum-character in favour of team performances. This could not be achieved by a new points system which fails to reward goal-scoring. Awarding a point for every goal would pep-up teams from the start to the finish of a season. There would be no point (literally) in settling for a goalless draw. Teams losing one—nil at Anfield come away persuading themselves they have won a moral victory. Not to lose by two or three goals is considered a magnificent performance.

Everyone, including chairmen and directors, agrees that the game is about scoring goals. Very well, let us make every goal count. I'm not impressed by people who pretend that they have enjoyed a goalless draw. I know from my experience in television that camera crews covering matches feel let-down when they come away without a goal in the can. The main matches chosen are nearly always those which have a fair quota of goals. A game without a goal is an anti-climax, regardless of the quality of mid-field play.

Good teams score goals and bad teams don't. It's as simple

as that. The system I suggest would not militate in any way against the sides which reach the top and challenge for the trophies under the present system. Why, then, change the system? The answer is that the game would be more competitive and positive in attack all the way through a League season.

Clubs unable to get near the championship contenders and already clear of the relegation zone, would not be tempted to ease off and let the rest of a season peter out. There would be something to fight for all the time and spectators would get what they demand and too infrequently get – attack, attack, attack!

There have been numerous suggestions from football supporters writing to the Press. Here is one from Mr A. Higgs, of Wordsley, near Stourbridge. He advocates: one point for a no-score draw, two points for a score draw, three points for a home win, four points for an away win.

While this suggestion has much to commend it and might well make football more entertaining and attractive, as he believes, a vital factor has been overlooked. Football is, or should be, a simple game. The less complicated it is, the better. Various permutations would only confuse players and spectators alike. No one wants to watch a game with a ready reckoner handy.

I can see no disadvantages with a straightforward point-a-goal system. If we do not try something new, we shall be stuck with old ideas which have lost their appeal and their momentum.

Ideas being discussed by club chairmen seem only to fudge the real issues. It is as if they feel they have to get together to 'look busy', that is all they seem to do! How can they discuss anything truly relevant when few, if any of them have even read the official reports on the game over the past few years?

I have made a point over the years when meeting club chairmen and directors in my capacity as PFA chairman of asking them whether they have read this or that report. Invariably, the answer is, 'No.' Here are the people who control the game, practically ignorant of the most important reports about it! No wonder the game is in such dire straits.

How can they learn anything when all they do is talk among themselves? They should be seeking the help and advice of the professionals in the game, the people in daily contact with all the problems, difficulties and issues. Chairmen and directors are away from their clubs most of the time, attending to their own business affairs. Now and again they come together for so-called seminars, a word which suggests leisurely, academic debate.

At their Solihull meeting the PFA was invited to send representatives, but they were present only as observers and were not able to contribute their views except on one topic. Were they afraid of being told what they did not want to hear?

When I asked at a meeting in July 1974, between the PFA and the FA disciplinary committee, why Trevor Morris, of the Welsh FA, was present, Bob Lord snapped, 'He's been invited here as an observer.' I was not against his presence, only against partiality. It was unfair for the Welsh FA to be represented when there was no representative of the Managers' and Secretaries' Association. So I suggested that at the next meeting, someone representing managers should be invited. After all, managers were concerned about disciplinary matters involving players. It was only reasonable that they be invited, if only as observers.

My manager at Wolves, Bill McGarry, who never could believe me when I told him that managers were all-important people in the game, went as a representative to a later disciplinary meeting, which illness prevented my attending. On his return he sent for me. He was fuming and complained he had been humiliated by having to sit there without saying anything. I told him that if it hadn't been for my intervention he would not have been there at all.

Before the end of the 1980–81 season, now being described as 'a crisis season' in the history of the game, joint meetings should have been held by chairmen in conjunction with representatives of all the football bodies to thrash out new structures, procedures and formats for getting the 1981–82 season off to a good start. Discussions of what is going wrong with the game have largely been confined to the sports columns. For their part, the chairmen have been content to sit back and let events take their course, while crucial issues are sidetracked by low-key discussions involving Sunday football and three points for a win.

'Would you like ice in your drink?' a steward asked a passenger as the Titanic struck the iceberg, and as the ship went down the orchestra's conductor called a conference to decide on the choice of final hymn.

Sick jokes sometimes point a moral, about futility and complacency. Football's sick joke is that those who could save a sinking ship are busying themselves with irrelevant, trivial issues and ignoring the iceberg. The 1980–81 season will be remembered not for radical decisions being made to halt decline and plan for the eighties, but for the abandonment of red and yellow cards. Even this was done in a clumsy, ill-judged manner, restoring the confusion the system was introduced to eliminate.

Television commentators shared the public's confusion in the first matches – FA Cup-ties – which followed the ending of the system. No one knew if a player had been booked or only lectured by a referee. Reporters had to scurry about afterwards to find out whose names had gone into the books.

Admittedly, the red and yellow cards had caused a great deal of ill-feeling and injustice. The fault lay in the way the system was operated, rather than in the system itself. Referees were not allowed to use their discretion. They were bound to send off a player booked twice for a misdemeanour. A player could be sent off for two minor offences in one game and be suspended, then go the rest of the season with no booking, while another player could be booked at least six times in different games and not be suspended.

Sometimes referees were caught in an embarrassing situation. Having booked a player for an offence, a referee could find himself reaching for his notebook after another offence and then find himself having to send off a player he had not immediately recognised as the one he had previously booked.

There were far too many sendings-off for comparatively trivial offences. Matters came to a head when Coventry defender Danny Thomas was sent off when booked twice in a Cup-tie against Leeds, after scoring the Sky Blues' goal. The system was seen to be working against itself and persistent criticism led the authorities to dispense with it. What they should have done is modify it.

Referees could have been instructed to send off players booked for committing the same offence more than once. A player guilty of different misdemeanours could be booked twice without being sent off. He would simply accumulate points. This would have resolved the dilemma to everyone's satisfaction. Instead, the authorities made a ham-fisted decision, getting rid of the cards altogether and plunging everyone back into confusion.

The introduction of the red and yellow cards served the same sort of purpose as the introduction, in the 1930s, of numbers on players' shirts – to enable spectators and the Press to identify players. I have been in favour of the red-and-yellow card system, as a means of clarification. All I was against was the gross unfairness in its application. Referees should have argued for its retention, with greater powers of discretion. Instead, without an autonomous association of their own which could have voiced their opinions, they meekly submitted to the FL's directive and the result is retrograde.

The decision to do away with the cards was hasty and was obviously taken in response to the build-up of criticism in the Press. Managers fumed against the injustices and everything came to the boil after particular sendings-off seen in televised games. When the 'big guns' blast off, the football authorities take notice.

It is amazing that this should have happened suddenly, when the same anomalies had been apparent for a number of seasons, since the system was introduced. If wiser counsels had prevailed, the FA and the PFA could have discussed the anomalies in the post-season review of disciplinary measures. Then, after careful consideration, new legislation could have been introduced in time for the new season to make sure the red and yellow card procedure was fairly and justly administered.

The FA's reaction to the 'sore thumb' sticking out of the upraised hand was to cut off the hand!

When will they ever learn to think, consider and act in co-operation with all interested parties? Was a meeting held between representatives of chairmen, managers, players and referees before the red and yellow card system was thrown out? If so, I did not hear of it. Were alternative ideas discussed? Was modification itself discussed with referees? If so, I did not hear.

It is just another example in a long list of ill-considered measures taken by the football authorities on behalf of others, whose true interests are not being properly represented.

The trouble is, of course, that the game is in the hands of dilettantes, whose lack of vision never ceases to amaze and confound me. We can take other examples at random. In the past long-term contracts have been drawn up with the pools promoters in advance, without allowing for inflation. Where is the sense in that? The 25 per cent taken by the company operating Wembley Stadium, from the proceeds of Cup Finals and international matches over the past ten years, is enough to build a new stadium – or at least to lay the foundations of one. The FA could have had all this money if it had bought the stadium twenty years ago and our national game would have had its own national centrepoint.

This is what I mean by lack of vision, which is simply having enough imagination to reflect and prepare for the future. All the time we are tripping over our bootlaces and scoring own goals. I could understand the paralysis which seems to have gripped the game if there were no options and no alternatives, if we really were in a cul-de-sac with a high wall at the end. The irony is that self-help measures are available and have been there, in the pages of various reports, for at least fifteen years.

I remember the shock I had at my farewell dinner at Wolves. The directors and manager attended the dinner held for me at the Victoria hotel. It coincided with the freedom of contract negotiations and minutes of the PFA negotiating committee had been sent to all the 92 League clubs. During the dinner I was astonished to discover that with the exception of John Ireland, the chairman, none of the directors had read them. How on earth were they supposed to keep themselves informed and discuss proposed changes if they did not consult the relevant documents?

After Bill McGarry left the dinner, before coffee was served, the directors listened to me until the early hours, telling them what was going on and why. They were better informed, if not converted, when they left the dinner.

How many directors, at the 92 League clubs, have negotiated with the Sports Council for grants to prepare multi-sports schemes? When I began negotiations with the Sports Council on behalf of Kettering Town, in 1976, we were the twenty-third club to have done so, but the others had fallen out, for various reasons. I had gratifying response, finding the Sports Council ready and eager to co-operate in the scheme to convert the ground into a sports complex. A considerable sum of money was promised, subject to essential conditions. It was only through lack of support in the town itself that the scheme failed to get off the drawing boards. While discussions were taking place, the scheme received much publicity and I had a letter from Eddie Plumley, then secretary of Coventry City FC, asking how I had gone about it. How delighted I was that such an eminent League club should come to me at a non-League club for advice. There was no secret. All they had to do, really, was ask the Sports Council for information. But it seemed, in outside eyes, that I was pioneering a scheme, which provoked interest and curiosity at League level. For the record, I did not tell Coventry City what they could easily have found out for themselves anyway. Schemes like this are not difficult to get underway, provided there is sufficient vision and commitment.

If there is an explosion, they will back away, murmuring, 'I could have told him it wouldn't work.' But when a new idea does work, they are quick to leap on the bandwagon. A lot of clubs remained quiet, on the sidelines, waiting for the outcome of my tussle at Kettering with the football authorities over sponsored jerseys. No one was prepared to stand at my side, until I had proved my point, that sponsorship was essential to bring more money into the game. Then, when all the fuss died down, sponsorship was accepted and is now a fact of footballing life. This is called 'pioneering', but in reality it is only responding to need, seeking ways of helping the game to help itself.

In this book I have ranged over and examined methods of re-structuring football so that it does not have to pitch from one crisis to another, with directors and managers wondering where the money is to come from, as attendances decline and the fans become more disenchanted. The crisis has been of football's own making; that is, created unwittingly by administrators and legislators who have failed to move with the times because their minds are conditioned by times gone by. They have inherited a system they feel obliged to perpetuate, because they cannot conceive another, more enterprising, system.

They have had their opportunities and they have spurned them. Instead of taking others into their confidence, the hierarchy have shown that their main concern is preserving vested interests. Then, when the roof starts to cave in, as at Crystal Palace, directors thrash about scarcely knowing what to do and the shenanigans make dramatic 'copy' for the newspapers, leaving players and supporters to become demoralised and bewildered.

The rot has set in, but it need not spread. It can be cut out of the system and the system itself re-vitalised by injections of new ideas and attitudes.

A salutary parallel can be found in another form of mass entertainment, the cinema. Over the years it has declined, to such an extent that many areas of the country which once had ten or 20 cinemas, are now without any. Families have stayed away in droves and attendances at British cinemas this year, 1981, are expected to be below 100 million, less than ten per cent of the attendance in 1950. For five years one man – he retired this Spring – had the power of deciding which films were shown in Rank cinemas. Between them, Rank and Thorn-EMI dictate the film programmes of 80 per cent of the country's cinemas. One or two men have absolute power in choosing what people who still go to the cinema, see on the screens. In view of falling attendances, one might have expected a new approach by the big circuits, with their virtual monopoly. But the same system has persisted, causing anger and frustration among those who want a more liberal and flexible film distribution system.

When a system becomes intransigent and works against the interests of those it is meant to serve, it should be dismantled. Football, like the cinema, is losing thousands of its previous enthusiasts. They are turning away in anger and frustration and they will not come back until they feel their interests are being properly represented, that those who control the game really care about them. They can only care about them by caring for the game, which is where I came in, brandishing my copy of the Chester Report.

Endpiece

I have tried to show in this book that professional football as I have known it, could perish before long unless a system in decay is replaced by more enlightened attitudes. I can well imagine someone reading these words and saying, 'It's easy to talk – and to write – what about some action? Who don't you get up from your typewriter and do something?'

This is precisely what I have been doing, between chapters of this book. After months of planning and research, towards the end of 1980 I submitted a report to Wolverhampton Borough Council on the feasibility of a multi-sports centre, by converting an existing but limited sports stadium at Aldersley, on the edge of the borough. I was prompted to devise the scheme by disillusionment over the failure of Wolverhampton Wanderers, in planning the reconstruction of its ground; to prepare any additional sports or recreational facilities. Having built a new Molineux Street stand, the club found itself hopelessly in debt, to the extent of paying almost £16,000 a month interest to the bank on a massive loan. All that is planned in the space below the stand are departments for the nearby Polytechnic, from which the club will get less than £50,000 a year rent. In my opinion, the entire project was misconceived from the start and I was not surprised when a third of the way through the 1980–81 season, the club announced that further phases had had to be postponed (did they mean abandoned?) through lack of money.

The ideal scheme I outlined to the local authority could serve as a prototype for other authorities, throughout the country. Here is the text of my introductory address to representatives of the borough council when they listened on the site to my proposals:

'According to the Book of Proverbs, where there is no vision, the people perish. It is a dramatic way of saying that without foresight, imagination and practical planning, a society stagnates.

'Ironically, in our technical society, which has made living so much easier than in the past and given people more leisure than our ancestors could have imagined, social stagnation has become widespread.

'Although more people are mobile than in the past and not rooted, most of the time, to their immediate neighbourhoods, there is a feeling of social frustration. Take away the television set and many people, young, middle-aged and elderly, say they do not know what to do with their time. In post-war years, the community spirit, which united the country in war-time, has almost fallen apart. People are no longer on close and friendly terms with their neighbours. In many instances, families do not even know their neighbours. Pride in community has declined and yet there is a desperate, underlying desire for restoration of community values. The trouble is, few people know how it can be achieved.

'The potential spirit is there, the means are lacking. But they need not be. Six years ago, an idealistic and hopeful government White Paper called on local authorities and football clubs to join forces in multi-sports centre schemes. They were urged to develop facilities for whole communities.

'Traditionally, football clubs have been inbred and self-contained, limiting their activities, primarily to Saturday afternoons, as far as the public are concerned. Asking them to change their concept of their role and responsibility to the local community and thereby to re-develop their grounds, in association with local authorities, is tantamount to asking them to revolutionise themselves. Such radical proposals take a long time to seep into the consciousness of football club chairmen and directors, who are more concerned with the problems of short-term finance.

'In the 1980's the whole of the United Kingdom faces a revolutionary decade. I am not talking about barricades in the streets, and the seizure of power by anti-capitalist forces. This, fortunately, is not in the mood and temper of the British people.

'But a social revolution is occurring and we need to plan urgently, to cope with the consequences. Failure to do so within the next few years will mean anger, frustration and possibly, more anti-social violence.

'Industrial recessions and the spread of highly sophisticated new technology means that before the end of the present decade, we shall have to accept, possibly, a 35-hour or a 30-hour week. It is inevitable that by the 1990's, men will have the option of retirement in their mid-fifties. Better nutrition and hygiene have helped to 'keep people young' in their fifites, when in previous generations people of that age would be feeling old.

'There will be millions of people, young, middle-aged and still in their prime in their fifties and sixties, in physical and mental need for ways to express themselves.

'Wolverhampton has the unique and ideal opportunity of serving as a prototype for communities throughout the United Kingdom. The project proposed, based at Wolverhampton Stadium, is far-reaching and, I think, visionary in its scope and purpose.

'It is not intended as "therapeutic" to act as an antidote for hooliganism, vandalism and other forms of anti-social behaviour. I do not claim that this project will automatically "cure" the afflictions of modern society. But I do claim that it will provide opportunities for the release of energy, for youngsters who might otherwise feel compelled to discharge their pent-up energies in hooliganism and vandalism.

'A social and communal atmosphere would be created to counteract the stagnation which is partly responsible for the demoralising aspects of life in an over-organised, but under-planned community.

'Young people with nothing to do, kick their heels and eventually kick one another.

'A multi-purpose sports and social centre, outgoing in its outlook and pitched well above the restrictive notion of a "members' club", would be a focal point for the community.

'I was the first person to advocate this sort of project while engaged as Chief Executive of Kettering Town FC. Negotiations took place with the Sports Council to finance the project, but for various reasons, associated with the football club, it did not get off the ground.

'The opportunity to enlarge on the idea is more propitious in Wolverhampton, with the existence of the very basis of a multi-sports centre, at Wolverhampton Stadium on the edge of the town, and with spacious countryside around. It is the ideal site for all that is envisaged.

'All manner of sports and recreations could be accommodated, including squash, badminton, five-a-side football, tennis, sauna, bowls . . . not that the entire emphasis would be on active sport. There would be social facilities, so that even those who are not sports-minded would feel at home and be able to enjoy the relaxed atmosphere.

'It is astonishing that between Crystal Palace and Brendan Foster's Gateshead, there is no place, apart from Cwmbran, in Wales, where people can deploy their athletic interests with adequate facilities.

'Inevitably, the likes of Brendan Foster, Steve Ovett and Sebastian Coe, will always come through, by virtue of sheer endeavour and initiative. But for every star of the track, there are hundreds who wish only to push themselves as far as they can go and enjoy athletics and sport, within their own limitations, at their own pace.

'The project I have outlined will enable them to do so and at the same time the local authority and community would be drawn together, in the common interest. From the age of 6 to the age of 90 (or older), young and not-so-young would find their interests not only served, but stimulated and developed. Everyone has need of social and physical diversion. This is self-apparent, but so far, while paying lip service to the need for such projects, no one has set about providing the facilities. Perhaps the task has appeared too complicated and immense. I can show that, with the co-operation and enthusiasm of the local authority, and the goodwill of a community, a project of this nature can be established simply and efficiently.

'I envisage a model, or prototype, which would have other authorities scurrying to Wolverhampton to study it and emulate it in their own areas.

'There is an old music-hall joke about Wolverhampton. A visitor arrives and asks someone, "What is there to do for excitement in this town?" and he is told. "You could go to the railway station and watch the shunting."

'Shunting aside complacency and indifference to the needs of the community, we now have a major opportunity of getting the town on the right social and sporting tracks, providing the means for "letting off steam" in the latter part of the twentieth century.

'It is elementary dynamics that pressure held down in one place will find its release in another, sometimes with disastrous results.

'A multi-sports centre, embracing varied social amentities, would channel the energies of thousands of people. It would also create civic pride and prestige, which are intangible but priceless assets for any community.

'The alternative is continued and worsening stagnation.'

28th November, 1980.

Main Sources

Government Papers:

1. PEP Report. Policy Studies Institute: English Professional Football, June 1966
2. Department of Education & Science: Report of the Committee on Football, 1968, commonly known as the Chester Report.
3. Commission on Industrial Relations: Report No. 87 on Professional Football (HMSO 1974).
4. White Paper on Sport, 1975 Denis Howell.
5. Royal Commission on Gambling Final Report 1978 (Command Paper 7200).

AND many other sources including the Sports Council, Sports Legislature and informal discussions with the Local Authority, Government and the media.